I R A N

I R A Q

Mosul

Arbil

Kirkuk

Halabja

Tikrit

Kifri

Samarra

★ Baghdad

Karbala ● Babylon
● Hindiyah

Tigris River

Najaf

Qal'at Sukkar ● Rifa

Euphrates River

Nasiriya ●

Basra ●

Zubayr ●

Rumelia ●
● Umm Qasr
Al Faw peninsula ●

K U W A I T

Kuwait City ★

**Satellite image taken on May 4, 2003, by NASA MODIS Rapid Response Team**

This book is to be returned on or before
the last date stamped below.

18 DEC 2007

# LIFE

# The
# War in Iraq

## THE ILLUSTRATED HISTORY

# LIFE

**Editor** Robert Sullivan
**Creative Director** Ian Denning
**Picture Editor** Barbara Baker Burrows
**Executive Editor** Robert Andreas
**Associate Picture Editors** Christina Lieberman, Vivette Porges
**Writer-Reporters** Hildegard Anderson (Chief), Anne Hollister, Peter Meyer, Carol Vinzant
**Art Director** Anthony Wing Kosner
**Assistant Picture Editors** Katherine Bourbeau, Dot McMahon, Lora Morgenstern
**Copy** JC Choi (Chief), Mimi McGrath, Wendy Williams
**Production Manager** Michael Roseman
**Picture Research** Lauren Steel
**Photo Assistant** Joshua Colow
**Consulting Picture Editors**
Suzanne Hodgart (London), Tala Skari (Paris)

**Publisher** Andrew Blau
**Director of Business Development** Marta Bialek
**Finance Director** Camille Sanabria
**Assistant Finance Manager** Karen Tortora

**Editorial Operations** Richard K. Prue (Director), Richard Shaffer (Manager), Brian Fellows, Raphael Joa, Stanley E. Moyse (Supervisors), Keith Aurelio, Gregg Baker, Charlotte Coco, Scott Dvorin, Kevin Hart, Rosalie Khan, Po Fung Ng, Barry Pribula, David Spatz, Vaune Trachtman, Sara Wasilausky, David Weiner

Special thanks to Marlene Adler, Jon C. Campbell and Dennis R. Hood (USGS)

**Time Inc. Home Entertainment**

**President** Rob Gursha
**Vice President, Branded Businesses**
David Arfine
**Vice President, New Product Development**
Richard Fraiman
**Executive Director, Marketing Services**
Carol Pittard
**Director, Retail & Special Sales** Tom Mifsud
**Director of Finance** Tricia Griffin
**Assistant Marketing Director** Ann Marie Doherty
**Prepress Manager** Emily Rabin
**Book Production Manager** Jonathan Polsky
**Associate Product Manager** Jennifer Dowell

Special thanks to Bozena Bannett, Robert Dente, Gina Di Meglio, Anne-Michelle Gallero, Peter Harper, Suzanne Janso, Robert Marasco, Natalie McCrea, Mary Jane Rigoroso, Steven Sandonato

Iconic images from the LIFE Picture Collection are now available as fine art prints and posters. The prints are reproductions on archival, resin-coated photographic paper, framed in black wood, with an acid-free mat. Works by the famous LIFE photographers—Eisenstaedt, Parks, Bourke-White, Burrows, among many others— are available. The LIFE poster collection presents large-format, affordable, suitable-for-framing images. For more information on the prints, priced at $99 each, call 888-933-8873 or go to www.purchaseprints.com. The posters may be viewed and ordered at www.LIFEposters.com.

Published by

# LIFE Books

Time Inc.
1271 Avenue of the Americas
New York, NY 10020

ISBN: 1-932273-13-1
Library of Congress Control Number: 2003106597
"LIFE" is a trademark of Time Inc.

We welcome your comments and suggestions about LIFE Books. Please write to us at: LIFE Books, Attention: Book Editors, PO Box 11016, Des Moines, IA 50336-1016

If you would like to order any of our hardcover Collector's Edition books, please call us at 1-800-327-6388 (Monday through Friday, 7:00 a.m.– 8:00 p.m. or Saturday, 7:00 a.m.–6:00 p.m. Central Time).

Please visit us, and sample past editions of LIFE, at www.LIFE.com.

**Half Title Page** The Kurdish population in the town of Kifri was shelled by the Iraqis.
FRANCESCO ZIZOLA/MAGNUM PHOTOS

**Title Page** On April 9, 2003, in Baghdad, a statue of Saddam Hussein stands in front of the National Olympic Committee building.
CAROLYN COLE/THE LOS ANGELES TIMES

**This Page** On January 17, 2003, the USS *Bonhomme Richard* prepares to depart San Diego for the Persian Gulf.
ERIC GRIGORIAN/POLARIS

# Pictures Worthy of Contemplation

## An Introduction by Walter Cronkite

In the propaganda that swirled around World War I there appeared the claim that this was "the war to end wars." It turned out that this was an empty promise and an impossible dream. The claim was made in an effort to justify a war so murderous and destructive that it offended all peoples including those who started it and those who saw it coming but failed to stop it.

Perhaps a similar claim should be made about the U.S.-Iraqi war that opened the 21st century. The escalation of the firepower with which nations could equip their military today cast an entirely new light on the face of war. The explosive power packed into bombs, the electronic precision with which they could be guided to their targets, pilotless airplanes and virtually indestructible tanks, television and computers that kept combat commanders advised of the exact location of friend and foe—it was Star Wars all right, but Star Wars transferred to Planet Earth.

No doubt about it—it was our first "push button" war. It must have alerted us by now to the danger that lurks in the future: the future President of the United States decides on war; the Constitution still being in effect, the Congress grants its approval; the lights go on in a special bunker under the White House basement as men and women in uniform take their places in front of television screens and panels of buttons; the red lights in front of them turn to green and they attack the buttons. The bombers are on their way, their deadly weapons already programmed to drop on the targets chosen perhaps weeks before, or possibly, in dire crisis, decided minutes earlier. World War III (or is it World War IV or V or VI) is underway.

At this point, in the late spring of 2003, only weeks after the Iraqi war, we haven't heard of the equally miraculous defensive weapons that presumably our military is planning, in the rare possibility that some other nation should match our push-button offensive capability. Yes, Star Wars lurks in the transistors that stand ready to answer the push-button signal from the Defense Command headquarters, perhaps in that White House basement bunker.

Meanwhile, as we begin to relax from the hours spent at our television sets we can review what we have just seen—the end of traditional warfare, the birth of war's modern age. The technological advances that changed the face of war also brought the war into our living rooms. That smacks of the phrase so often spoken during the Vietnam War: Television was bringing the war to the nation's dinner tables. That reference was to the fact that the three television networks of the time included in their dinnertime news summaries, film taken one to three or four days earlier of action in the forests and the fields of the Vietnam battleground. The motion pictures, taken by daring camera crews in the heart of the combat, had been flown to the United States to be developed and edited before reaching the TV screens. The Iraqi war, in contrast, was brought to the nation's dinner tables in real time. We watched as the bombs exploded in glorious color on Baghdad's palaces. We saw and heard frontline war correspondents give us the play-by-play report as artillery blasted and small-arms fire rattled in the background.

This presentation of the Iraqi war was made possible by technological progress and the courtesy of the Defense Department. Stung by what many superior officers believed was television's part in turning many Americans against the Vietnam War, the military had banned reporters and photographers from accompany-

> As we begin to relax from the hours spent at our television sets we can review what we have just seen.

**Squad leader Sgt. Lonnie Roberts weeps for one of his men, the late Pvt. Gregory R. Huxley Jr., at a memorial service in Baghdad.**

ing the troops in its subsequent military incursions in Panama and Grenada and the real war of the Persian Gulf. In Gulf War I, it even insisted that an officer be present when the rare permission was granted to interview a soldier or two.

The blackout left the nation without an independent history and with only the military's own version of the first war with Iraq. In the ensuing years there was a drumbeat, insistent if not particularly noisy, from individuals and news organizations offended and deeply concerned by the Pentagon's denial of the people's right to know how their military performed in their name.

Whether because of these complaints or the political nature of the Iraqi commitment, the Pentagon reversed itself for Iraqi War II. Recognizing the capabilities of satellite communications, the Pentagon performed the almost impossible task of simultaneously opening up and restricting access of war correspondents

to the combat troops. It invented the ingenious concept of embedment: the assignment by the military of accredited correspondents to specific units. The correspondents were pledged to remain with those units for the duration and to obey whatever restrictions on coverage the commander of the unit felt necessary for operational security. With those restrictions, the correspondents and camera operators were permitted access to satellites to relay to the States their reports, in real time, as the action took place.

This was in sharp contrast to the press coverage during World War II and Vietnam. In World War II, in the great land battles of Europe, accredited correspondents and photographers were free to roam the entire battlefront with the key restriction that their copy or pictures had to be cleared by censors to avoid the inadvertent revelation to the enemy of military secrets. The system worked extraordinarily well.

# History to be absorbed and contemplated is found in pictures that we can examine and study. Photographs found in a book.

In Vietnam, correspondents could accompany troops to wherever they could hitch a ride, and there was no censorship. Since nearly all combat was between small units and there were no mass movements, there were few military secrets to be revealed. That system—or lack of one—kept the American public well informed of our soldiers' problems, their setbacks and their heroism. The candor did not set so well with the military leadership, leading to those post-Vietnam vows that the press would be contained in any future conflict.

The Pentagon's new policy for Iraq II led to the accreditation of more than 2,000 reporters, photographers and camera operators. The large majority was assigned to cover Central Command headquarters in Qatar, and, indeed, the Pentagon spent an estimated $250,000 building a state-of-the-art theater, designed by a Hollywood Art Director, for daily press briefings.

Some 600 correspondents and camerapeople were "embedded" with the combat troops. Many saw action while some were disappointed to find that the units to which they were assigned saw little actual combat. Ten journalists were killed in action, two are still missing, and four died of natural causes, including NBC's much-admired David Bloom.

In the first blush of victory while the correspondents were still embedded, it seemed that the military and the press agreed that the system had worked well. Indeed, during the war few complaints were heard that commanders had restricted the reporting of those attached to their units. What problems there were will see the light in months and years ahead as the inevitable books pour from the reporters' computers.

As to the war itself, as one of the commanding generals said to the chagrin of his superiors, the war they found was not the war they had trained for. Almost in the earliest hours as the American forces left their Kuwait staging areas and crossed into Iraq proper, they claimed to have liberated with scarcely a shot their first towns. Those claims had to be withdrawn as irregular Iraqi forces staked their own claims on those villages.

From there north to Baghdad it was to be a series of sometimes brief if intensive firefights as the American forces encountered the Fedayeen, the irregular but fierce forces loyal to Saddam who fought to defend towns, crossroads and vital bridges.

Perhaps provoked by the small scale of the action, retired American generals began popping up on television talk shows, criticizing the overall battle plan. In particular they feared that the United States had not committed a large enough force to overcome the vaunted Iraqi Republican Guard divisions that presumably were waiting for the Americans in Baghdad.

Probably the Iraqis' morale was shattered by the heavy precision bombing of the capital itself and the unchallenged and devastating air attacks on their own forces, but whatever the cause, the Iraqi Army virtually faded into the desert. It simply disappeared along with its leader, Saddam Hussein, himself.

As American troops swept into Baghdad virtually unopposed, victory was assured. It had been accomplished with the loss of 137 American troops and 32 British, tragic but not nearly as costly as many had anticipated. The Iraqi loss had not even been estimated weeks after the fighting, but it was believed to be in the thousands, both military and civilian.

The greatest concern of the American leadership had been that the allied forces would have to battle street-by-street, building-by-building through the crowded metropolis of Baghdad before securing victory. With the disappearance of the Republican Guard, that was not necessary, but as well prepared as the American leadership was for war, it turned out it was not nearly so well prepared for peace. American troops were met in Baghdad's streets not by hostile troops but by a civilian population apparently turned bitter and hostile by the riots and looting of their own making and the clear absence of an American plan to police the conquered city. The disorder provided another tableau for American photographers, this one buttressing the already existing worry over the nation's future in a conquered land.

But despite all of those exciting, riveting television reports from daring correspondents and camerapeople there was something missing, something very precious. It was the luxury of thoughtful contemplation.

The problem with the moving picture is that it moves. We are inclined to cry out as the camera sweeps over a complicated scene: "Hold it! Wait a minute! Stop there! What was that fellow in the foreground holding? What's going on there in the back?"

History is, undoubtedly, richly illuminated as it is captured by the television cameras, but the history to be absorbed and contemplated is to be found in those pictures we can examine and study at our leisure, the photographs to be found within the binding of a book.

**In Baghdad on April 7, 2003, a combat engineer with the U.S. Army's 3rd Infantry Division stands on a portrait of Saddam Hussein.**

# This Is Iraq

## An often-persecuted land is delivered to the 20th century, where fresh travails await.

It has been the nurturing place for sublime artistic and intellectual advancements, and it has been a place where raiders ransacked cultural treasures and rulers prohibited free thought. It has benefited the world immensely and then, in poor thanks, been overrun by some of the world's most vicious tyrants. It has allowed religions to grow and prosper, then seen religious strife lead to unspeakable atrocities within its ever fluid borders. While ceding due respect to other ancient, hallowed traditions, Iraq can claim to have been the birthplace of Adam, Eve and Noah, the patriarch Abraham and therefore his descendant monotheistic faiths (Judaism, Christianity and Islam), as well as arts and institutions ranging from writing to algebra to banking to social justice to war. If the time frame extends to the ancient, then it is fair to say no other place has experienced what Iraq has known, or has been as sig-

**The Sumerians were a cultured, inventive and polytheistic people. Abu was their god of vegetation.**

nificant in the course of human events.

Well before advanced civilizations blossomed in Egypt, Greece and Rome, there were the Sumerians, who farmed the lush fields in the Fertile Crescent between the Tigris and Euphrates rivers. Beginning about 4000 B.C., they developed irrigation systems, rules of law that allowed private ownership, such innovations as the wheel and the plow, a mathematics based on the number 60 that remains the basis for time measurement in the modern world, and even a mode of writing and recording. Cuneiform impressions made on clay with a reed stylus told of transactions within the community; by 3000 B.C., there was a full syllabic alphabet and, later, literature, the most famous example being the epic tale of Gilgamesh. So very much from bygone eras resonated in the recent war: Cuneiform tablets were among the many items that were lost when Iraq's National Museum was looted in the aftermath of Baghdad's liberation.

Iraq—the historical Mesopotamia—was a more democratic, "civilized" place than nations rising around it. In Egypt, for instance, the Pharaoh was all-powerful, and everyone was his soldier, serf or slave. By contrast, Mesopotamian kings answered to their people, if not strictly to an electorate, and did not seek to compete with the gods.

This earthly paradise would not last. The Sumerians were overcome in the 3rd century B.C., by a Semitic people from the Arabian peninsula. But several centuries later, King Hammurabi not only reunited the Sumerian tribes, he also extended their domain—his empire—north through the Tigris and Euphrates valleys and west to the Mediterranean. This was Babylonia, ruled from the city of Babylon, where, early in Hammurabi's reign, the king set forth an extraordinary code of law. It demanded justice even for the poor, and that punishment fit the crime ("an eye for an eye, a tooth for a tooth" was, literally, written in stone). After Hammurabi died in 1750 B.C., war returned to the region. Without listing all the changes in power, or the redrawings of boundaries, the point is: This region of the Middle East, with Iraq and its cities—Ur (where Abraham was born), Babylon and, later, Baghdad—contributed tremendously to the rise of civilization as we know it.

It continued to do so for centuries, under kings who were at least as draconian as they were progressive. Nebuchadrezzar ruled from Babylon, as did Nebuchadrezzar II, who built one of the world's Seven Wonders, the Hanging Gardens, and oversaw a golden age. Alexander the Great conquered in 331 B.C., and much later, in 1258 A.D., Genghis Khan's grandson, Hulegu, stormed Baghdad with 200,000 Tartars; Iraq became a forlorn outpost of a Mongol empire ruled from Iran. In 1535, Sultan Suleiman the Magnificent vanquished Baghdad and established an Ottoman rule that would, after some early instability, endure into the 20th century. The modern period has seen British Empire surrogates and, then, military strongmen ruling from Baghdad. The most famous and most despotic of these, Saddam Hussein, took to comparing himself to the Iraqi legends Hammurabi, Nebuchadrezzar II and Alexander.

Top: Scala/Art Resource; Erich Lessing/Art Resource; Iraq Museum/Bridgeman Art Library

**Other treasures from the National Museum in Baghdad: a vase from ancient Ur (circa 2450 B.C.), a head from Nineveh (2350 B.C.) and a tablet with cuneiform writing (1830 B.C.–1530 B.C.).**

While this parade of conquerors helps us understand Iraq's complex past, more crucial still to this understanding is one seminal moment in the country's religious history. The inspiring life of Muhammad, an Arab born in the desert city of Mecca circa 570, very quickly gave rise to the world's third great monotheistic faith: Islam, the religion of the Muslims. Allah-worshiping Arab Muslims grew in number to challenge the Hebrews and Christians of the north. The Persian tribes in what is now Iraq were mainly Christian when the Muslim campaigns began in 634. The invading Arab warriors, fighting a *jihad,* proved overwhelming even when outnumbered, and soon offered ultimatums to those they overran: "Accept the faith and you are safe; otherwise pay tribute. If you refuse to do either, you have only yourself to blame. A people is already upon you, loving death as you love life." At first some paid the tax and kept their religion. Over time, as intermarriage between Iraqis and Arabs created a new race, the inculcation of Islam was irresistible. Arabic replaced Persian as the standard tongue.

Subsequently, whatever

**Alexander (above) was a warrior king. Hammurabi was a lawgiver. Both were cited by Saddam Hussein as most worthy role models.**

Top: Scala/Art Resource; Erich Lessing/Art Resource

caliph, dictator or colonial administrator might try to govern Iraq would need to deal with an Islamic populace. The difficulty of this task depended on whether he chose to ignore or embrace Allah. Saddam Hussein, as a pertinent example, was a military dictator who tried to portray himself as a serious and important man of Islam. Meanwhile, he revealed himself, even to the subjugated and increasingly noneducated masses, as a fraud. Consider: In the year 680, Imam Hussein, an early spiritual leader of the Shiite Islamic sect, was killed in Karbala, and for centuries Shiites made an annual mass pilgrimage to honor the martyr. For 25 years, Saddam Hussein banned the pilgrimage. What kind of holy man is this? the Shiites asked themselves. The fervent worshipers who returned to Karbala in April 2003 knew for certain that an era of religious repression had ended.

Islamic Iraq has seen glory days: The 8th and 9th centuries were a kind of Islamic Renaissance, with the House of Wisdom rising in Baghdad, classical works from Plato to Pythagoras being rendered in Arabic, and the Baghdadi mathematician Abu Ja'far Muhammad ibn Musa al-Khawarizmi bequeathing to the world algebraic equations. And Islamic Iraq has seen times of strife: Through the centuries, debates about Islamic revelation have exacerbated divides even within Islam. This is why the big tent of the Muslim world has its sects—Shiite, Sunni—just as there are different forms of Christianity and orthodoxies within Judaism.

This last point vis-à-vis Iraq's Muslims was essentially overlooked when the long rule of the Ottomans came to an end with World War I, and Britain then forsook its promise to return the territory to its natives, instead staying as a colonial overlord. The map of Iraq that emerged in 1920 looked like a solid, large country—about the size of California—smack in the center of the cradle of civilization. But, in fact, the southern tier of the nation was peopled by a Shiite Muslim majority that was in conflict with the Sunni Muslim minority of the middle region. And in the northern province of Mosul, which Britain had sliced from Turkey and attached to Iraq, lived a non-Arab people, the Kurds, who generally embraced Islam but retained their own ethnic identity and language. Over this roiling citizenry, Britain installed a king.

By the time that situation devolved to Saddam Hussein, the reigning force in Baghdad was Saddam's Baath Party, which was aligned with the minority Sunnis. The Baaths would try to control the majority below and insurgents above through intimidation and murder. With this brutal formula, they—he—would try to solve the complications that are Iraq. And they—he—would try to conquer other lands, as Iraqi rulers had so long ago. Thus began another dramatic chapter in Iraq's often triumphant, often tragic history.

**Muhammad ascends in this Persian rendering from the 16th century. The prophet is always veiled, for to depict his face is to presume the role of Allah.**

# Baghdad 1958

A dramatic, bloody coup set wheels in motion
that led to the rise of Saddam Hussein.
LIFE photographer Larry Burrows was there.

In the sweltering summer of
'58, as the military toppled a
monarchy, Burrows recorded
an oil-supply fire that had been
set on the city's outskirts.
It is one of several shots that,
now, eerily echo images from
the Baghdad spring of 2003.

After millennia of being riven by religious and political strife—drawn and redrawn as Mesopotamia, part of Persia then the Ottoman Empire, dominated by giants from Alexander the Great to Suleiman the Magnificent—the land that we know as Iraq ought to have been prepared for whatever would befall it in the 20th century. Or so one would have thought. But no country could have been ready for such reversals of fate and fortune. One day it was ruled by a colonizing empire, now by a puppet king, now by a monarchy, now by a military dictatorship. The transitions in power were, as a rule, effected through violence. And always, beneath it all, the Muslim population seethed, divided within itself but often united in its detestation of whoever was ruling in Baghdad.

If the century was a microcosmic view of Iraqi history, with foreign conquerors coming and going and royal rulers ceding to military ones, then the events of 1958 were a critical fulcrum upon which the century balanced. After 1958 the path for Saddam Hussein was, if not wide open, at least clear.

The Ottomans, who had controlled Iraq since the 16th century, were still in charge in the early 20th, but as we have seen, their empire ended with World War I, and the occupying British cobbled together present-day Iraq. King Faisal I's monarchy was established under British protection in 1921, and Iraq gained its independence in 1932. Shortly after, the modern tradition of military coups d'état began: There were no fewer than seven in that decade, with Faisal's son and successor, King Ghazi, retained as a figurehead throughout. In 1939, Ghazi died in a car crash. His son, Faisal II, became a king at age three.

Many Muslims chafed under all this, especially after Great Britain reoccupied Iraq for the duration of World War II. Postwar bitterness against the West festered, much of it directed against Faisal II, whose reign was propped up by the British. In Iraq's military in particular there were men in thrall to Egypt's Gamal Abdel Nasser and his calls for Arab nationalism. Two such men were Brig. Gen. Abdel Karim Kassem and Col. Abdul Salam Arif. On July 14, 1958, they moved against Faisal II. The ancient rules still obtained: The boldest, most ruthless guy wins. The rest of the century would be gunslinger against gunslinger, and Saddam Hussein had a gun.

**Military coups were old hat to the new Iraq, but one in which a military man not only had a king killed but created for himself a premiership sent a powerful message. Kassem (opposite, having taken over, and above) told LIFE, "I am no dictator"—but he looked like one. Shortly after his coup, he split from Nasser's Arab crusade and, casting about for allies, found them among communists. Arif (below, right) was by Nasser's side in 1958, and remained loyal through '63, when he engineered Kassem's assassination.**

Kassem and Arif
insisted that their
men had shot back
only when engaged,
but Burrows's photos
speak of vengeful
violence and looting
similar to what would
follow, 45 years
later, the downfall
of Saddam Hussein.
Faisal II and family
were killed and their
palace, seen here,
sacked. The king's
prime minister,
Nuri al-Said, a deaf
old man but a survivor
of 37 years in office,
was even more
detested. The mob
hacked at his corpse.

The 1955 Baghdad Pact, signed by Faisal II, had decreed Iraq the West's ally, fanning hatred among a nationalistic Arab citizenry. Glee at the success of Arif and Kassem (above) was therefore general. Soon, however, other Arabs questioned Kassem's loyalties. Arif fell out, and so did the young activist Saddam Hussein, who in 1959 took part in a Bonnie-and-Clyde attack on the premier (below). Kassem survived; so did Saddam. Other intrigues—other coups—followed. One of them would elevate Arif. One would anoint Saddam.

Polaris

# Saddam Hussein

His reign was terrible, horrific, passionate, diabolical.
His downfall came too late for many.

**O**ne of the most durable dictators of the 20th century, he ruled an ancient people with cunning and cruelty for 24 years, managing not only a populace of warring tribes and ethnic federations but also a region simmering with political enmity and international consequence. He has been compared to Stalin for the efficiency of his state-sponsored terror machine, to Hitler for his megalomania and dreams of foreign domination, and to Tito for his ability to impose order on unruly provinces.

The machine, the dreams and the political deftness served Saddam Hussein well for a long time. Exacting obedience through terror and torture, with occasional reward weighed against the constant possibility of punishment, he kept 24 million Iraqis in check for decades—and most of the world at bay. His nemesis was the United States, which he continuously blamed for unjust treatment of Arab nations. He claimed America was responsible for Iraq's tragic want after the 1991 Gulf War, and said his country must be avenged.

**It is not an exaggeration to say that Saddamic tribute—statues, murals, plinths—could be found on most city blocks in Iraq prior to April 9, 2003. The messages: Uncle is great. He is always watching.**

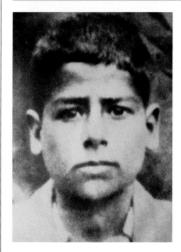 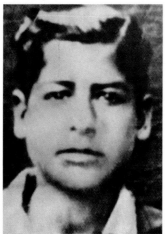  

He could be silver-tongued and charming, or fiercely blunt, but behind either mien he was brutally tough. From his 1959 participation, at age 22, in the assassination attempt on Iraqi premier Abdel Karim Kassem to the ultimate 2003 war strategy of using unarmed women and children as shields for his troops, Saddam showed himself to be ruthless. He earned a reputation—a reputation integral to the terror—as a keen and smiling serial killer, a hardworking mass murderer, one easy to hate and one to whom hate came easy. Biographer Said K. Aburish, who knew Saddam, subtitled his study *The Politics of Revenge.* Indeed, in Aburish's telling and that of others, it seemed that Saddam's life was dedicated to retribution for some primal wound. Like Homer's Achilles: "An angry man—there is my story."

Raised in an Iraqi village community that was permeated by instability, dishonesty and crime—where economic and social might was available to those who would seize it and hold it—Saddam came by his hallmark traits naturally. Even the day of his birth, long cited as April 28, 1937 (a date that, for the first time in years, recently passed uncelebrated as an Iraqi holiday), may be based on a lie. It has been said that Saddam fabricated a somewhat older self to avoid the taboo of having married a woman who was his senior, a violation of Arab custom.

It has also been speculated that Saddam's birth was a very near thing, that his mother, depressed by the deaths of her husband and son, attempted to kill herself while pregnant, then tried to abort the fetus—stopped both times by caring Jewish

**In 1963, the year Saddam returned to Iraq from exile in Egypt, he wed his cousin Sajida Khairallah Tulfah. Saddam sometimes strayed, and at one point had Sajida's brother, Adnan, killed, but—legally, at least—the marriage survived.**

neighbors. The details are sketchy, but we know that she did give birth to a fatherless boy and named him Saddam, an uncommon Arabic appellation that means, in one translation, "one who confronts."

In al-Awja, a village of mudbrick huts a hundred miles north of Baghdad, Saddam faced a rough existence from the beginning. The desolate country in the Iraqi badlands was matched by the harshness of young Saddam's home life. His job was to work in the fields, which he did barefoot, as his family had no money for shoes. His mother, Subha, married a cousin, Hassan Ibrahim, known as Hassan the Liar, partly for a locally famous boast of having made a pilgrimage to Mecca (a conceit that would pale next to his stepson's

From left: Gamma (2):Polaris; Getty

eventual claim of being descendant from the prophet Muhammad). Hassan's clan had cheats and thieves in its number, and Hassan was an idler who would spend hours in the village coffeehouse, meanwhile sending his stepson to steal chickens or even sheep. Hassan and Subha had several other boys who, by Arabic custom, enjoyed higher standing in the family than their stepbrother. In the one-room hut, which had no electricity or running water, things were bad for all, a life of overarching poverty and regular violence, but things were worst for Saddam. "I don't want him, the son of a dog," Hassan would shout.

Saddam escaped from it all by running away at age 10. He found safe harbor at the house of his mother's brother, Khairallah Tulfah, in the village of al-Shawish. Despite the facts of his early years, the adult Saddam always cited the larger, nearby town of Tikrit as his birthplace. It was there the dictator would build some of his most opulent palaces as well as a shrine to his mother. By claiming Tikriti heritage, he would align himself with the revered 12th century sultan Saladin, who actually was from Tikrit. Saddam, a consummate, calculating fabricator of legend, would establish his bona fides—as a transcendent Muslim, as a great Arab leader—by concocting a parallel reality. And there would be no quarrel with the Saddamic version, at least not in public.

If Saddam learned anger and violence at the hands of his stepfather, he learned bitterness at the knee of his uncle Khairallah, a cashiered army officer who sent the young Saddam to school. Khairallah had taken part, in 1941, in a failed

**After yet another overthrow—and once again finding himself on the wrong side of the ruling regime—Saddam (below, left) enjoys a prison term in 1965 that seems anything but arduous.**

coup against the ruling monarchy of young King Faisal II. He was arrested and lost his commission. Now he passed his political grievances, which extended backward to the British occupation of Iraq following World War I, on to Saddam. How grateful Saddam was for Khairallah's wisdom would later be reflected in President Hussein's first naming his uncle an honorary Iraqi general and then the mayor of Baghdad. For good measure, Saddam would make Khairallah's son, Adnan, chief of staff of the army and minister of defense.

Although he finished intermediate school, Saddam was refused entry to Baghdad's Military Academy owing to poor grades. He enrolled instead in 1955 in the al-Karkh secondary school, which was known as an incubator of nationalism.

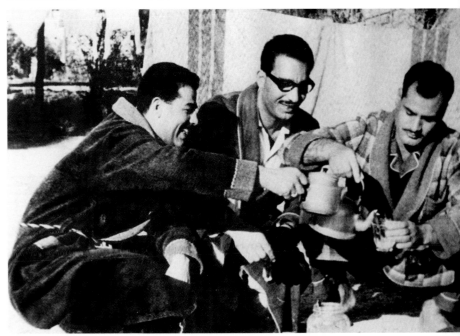

Gamma

There, Saddam began his involvement with the Baath Party, a socialist group founded in Syria and one of the first of many formed around the cause of Arab independence, a crusade that would be championed in the Middle East in the next several years by, most prominently, Egypt's Gamal Abdel Nasser. Thus, still a teenager, Hussein yoked his childhood rage to a political ideology that gave his anger a purpose and his loneliness a home. In 1956, when he was just 19 (younger, if you accept the altering of his birth date), he took part in a coup attempt against Faisal II and longtime prime minister Nuri al-Said. Though the coup failed, it marked the Baath Party as worthy of note, perhaps even fear, and Saddam as a political activist. Shortly thereafter he killed his brother-in-law for being a communist, though some believe Saddam invented this story. Either way, his became a bantered name in the volatile world of Iraqi politics.

Shots were often taken at the king and al-Said, and as we have seen in the preceding chapter, Faisal II was finally overthrown, his family and prime minister brutally dispatched, in July 1958. Military strongman Kassem took control, but it was quickly clear that he was not pushing any Baathist agenda, and in 1959, Saddam, by then a thug of some experience as well as a firebrand, took part in the daring daylight ambush of

**Whether swearing on the Koran at his 1979 inauguration or paying tribute during his 1976 pilgrimage to Mecca, Saddam's claims as a holy man were consistently belied by his deeds.**

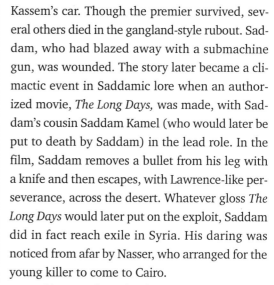

Kassem's car. Though the premier survived, several others died in the gangland-style rubout. Saddam, who had blazed away with a submachine gun, was wounded. The story later became a climactic event in Saddamic lore when an authorized movie, *The Long Days,* was made, with Saddam's cousin Saddam Kamel (who would later be put to death by Saddam) in the lead role. In the film, Saddam removes a bullet from his leg with a knife and then escapes, with Lawrence-like perseverance, across the desert. Whatever gloss *The Long Days* would later put on the exploit, Saddam did in fact reach exile in Syria. His daring was noticed from afar by Nasser, who arranged for the young killer to come to Cairo.

Saddam, under a death sentence in Iraq, was welcomed into a vibrant community of likethinkers from several Arab states who were holed up together in Egypt. He received a government stipend to finish his preparatory schooling, then enrolled at the University of Cairo Law School. In 1963 the Baathists back home, certainly with Nasser's implicit if not complicit support, conspired with former Kassem sidekick Abdul Salam Arif to successfully assassinate Kassem. Saddam returned to Iraq and immediately got busy, helping Arif to execute more than 700 people.

Saddam was married that same year to a cousin, Sajida Khairallah Tulfah, daughter of the man who had raised him. The bride received an

early taste of what was in store when the Baathists were overthrown and a hunt was on for her new husband among others. Saddam added to the luster of his reputation for brave revolutionary action when, in a shoot-out, he kept his adversaries at bay until his ammo ran out. While in prison, he was elected to a leadership post in the Baath Party, for whatever short-term good it did him. He read assiduously while in jail—Hemingway's *The Old Man and the Sea* was a favorite—and he plotted. In 1966 he escaped and went into hiding. On the lam, he fell in with fellow Baathists, and in 1968 the party rose up once more to topple the government. Saddam donned a military uniform for this coup, and rode into Baghdad on a tank.

In reward for his years of bravery and service, and still only 32 at most, Saddam was made Iraqi vice president as well as deputy chairman of the new government's ruling Revolutionary Command Council. That same year, he earned his law degree, or at least was granted it; one report is that he showed up for his final exams wearing a pistol in his belt and accompanied by four armed

**Wearing the mask: In Baghdad in 1983, Saddam returns a salute with a smile. In March 1988 in the northern Iraq town of Halabja, home to more than 70,000 ethnic Kurds, an horrific genocide is perpetrated when Iraqi jets drop several kinds of poison gas, killing 5,000 innocents.**

He always dressed the part, whether sitting with Saudi Arabia's King Fahd or embracing Yasir Arafat (bottom left) of the Palestine Liberation Organization or Jordan's King Hussein. He dressed for these roles, and was usually acting, false promises coming to his lips as readily as condemnations of Western infidels. Unless, of course, the infidels were of use to him . . .

bodyguards. The methodology of might that had served Saddam during his adolescence in an outlaw village community would now be pursued, in spades, during his long career in the city.

In the decade following the Baath ascendancy, Saddam, always a workhorse, toiled with such purposefulness that he came to be regarded by those in and around the government as the real ruling power, President Ahmed Massan al-Bakr notwithstanding. Saddam had read admiringly not only of Hemingway's stoic Santiago but also of the Soviet chairman Joseph Stalin; now he emulated that tyrant by putting in 18-hour days and taking on as many jobs as he could, including key roles in the internal security and intelligence agencies. Saddam took charge of the Peasants Department, the committee controlling relations with the always troublesome Kurds and the one overseeing dealings with other Arab states. He angled for control of the country's oil industry. Saddam was in play everywhere during this period, exhibiting "amazing willpower, amazing focus," in the appraisal of biographer Aburish, who would become a consultant to Saddam's own government once it was formed.

Strong now, Saddam flexed his muscles, although not often in the diabolical fashion for which he would become infamous. In fact, he appeared throughout the '70s to be something of a progressive. With control of the world's second-largest petroleum reserves, he enriched himself and his kin, yes, but also funneled enormous sums of money to a modernization of Iraq's infrastructure. He launched a nationwide literacy program, improved higher education and set up one of the best public-health systems in the Middle East. His reputation beyond Iraq's borders was positive and growing; the United Nations awarded him a UNESCO citation for his humanitarianism, and Saddam had cordial meetings with Washington diplomats as well as those from Arab nations.

Even before he eased the ailing al-Bakr out of office in 1979, Saddam was placing family members and other badlands cronies—what would become known as the Tikrit Mafia—in key government positions. When he did assume the presidency, his authority was absolute, his gang formidable, and, inside Baghdad, his ruthlessness well-known. Those who had been sentenced to

**. . . in which case he doffed the headgear and practiced his handshake. He gladly accepted arms from both the U.S.S.R. (top, with General Secretary Leonid Brezhnev in Moscow in 1977) and the U.S. (Baghdad, '83, with White House envoy Donald Rumsfeld).**

three years in prison for skipping the literacy program realized that behind Saddam the Beneficent stood Saddam the Tyrannical.

If any doubted the new leader's power, their doubts were soon dispelled. Almost immediately after succeeding al-Bakr, Saddam called a party meeting and, calmly smoking a cigar as he talked, began to detail a plot launched in Syria to undermine the Iraqi government. He started naming "traitors" among Baath Party cohorts (and potential rivals) who were present. They were escorted from the room, one by one, 60 in all. Those who remained, fearful for their lives, shouted fealty to their president. Saddam's henchmen disseminated a videotape of the tumultuous meeting among Iraqi officials and on the streets to make sure the message was clear. The postscript circulated too: Weeks after the meeting, 22 of the alleged plot-

The patriarch: Saddam and his wife, Sajida, enjoy barbecued kebabs with their extended family. Below: Son Uday feeds a pet. The photo at left, in particular, and other candids found after the fall of Baghdad in April 2003, speak to the banality of evil in the same fashion that shots of Hitler in his Alpine retreat did a half century earlier.

ters were executed.

It was only the first of President Hussein's periodic purges. At a cabinet meeting in 1982, for instance, he asked his health minister, Riyadh Ibrahim, to accompany him outside. It seemed bad penicillin had been issued to the army, and someone had to pay. According to Aburish, Saddam shot Ibrahim in an anteroom, then returned to the meeting. Saddam, for his part, was unapologetic about his Stalinesque exercise of power. When asked by one courageous European reporter if reports of reprisal, torture and death had any basis in fact, Saddam replied, "Of course. What do you expect if they oppose the regime?" In Tikrit, in one of Saddam's favorite movies, *The Godfather,* and now in Baghdad, mafioso justice was not only comprehensible, it was also justifiable.

In foreign affairs, before Saddam resorted to the gun, duplicity was his modus operandi. Consider: Following the 1969 Baath takeover, Saddam purged all communists from the government, then visited Moscow to negotiate an arms deal that was supposed to last 15 years. Six years in, President Hussein, trying to curry favor with the U.S., ordered the execution of 21 communists in the Iraqi military. In 1978 and '79, some 7,000 Iraqi

communists reportedly disappeared.

Consider the 1975 Algiers Treaty. While embroiled in a Kurdish uprising in the north, Saddam signed a pact with Iran securing the Shah's promise to end his support of the Kurds, thereby clearing a path to a frightful Kurdish genocide. In 1980, firmly in control, but with a Shiite Ayatol-

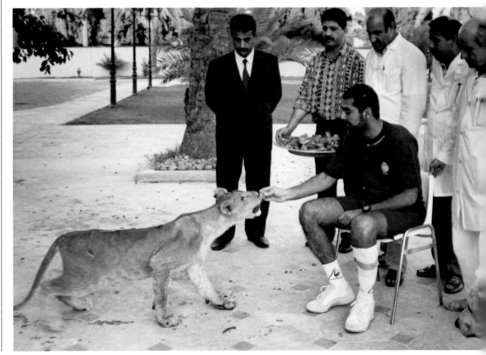

lah having replaced the Shah, Saddam abrogated the pact by attacking Iran. The subsequent eight-year war would end in stalemate and cross-border devastation, but it provided Saddam with an ancillary benefit as it made him a favorite in Washington. Huge supplies of arms were shipped to Baghdad to help in its fight against the Ayatollah who had, in 1979 and '80, held Americans—and America—hostage. "Everybody in the whole wide world wants to know more about the president and his incredible achievements, and how he is standing up to the devil in Tehran," said Terence Young. And who was Terence Young? He was the director of several James Bond films, and had been hired to work on the six-hour version of *The Long Days,* the propagandistic biopic about Saddam's early years. Young was part of a strategy to portray Saddam as a brave revolutionary rather than an expansionist dictator. What went unpublicized by Saddam's PR machine was that the dictator's eyes were resolutely trained on a pan-Arab universe dominated by him alone, a nationhood that could and would defy the West. He was the man who would be Nasser.

When did things begin to unravel for him? Certainly the long war with Iran did not help. The progress that Iraq had made under Baath Party rule was erased, and the country was left thoroughly broken—but with a massive army, fourth largest in the world. Well before Saddam, Iraq had made claims on small, oil-soaked Kuwait just to its southeast. In 1990, he turned the one thing he had remaining, military might, on the all-but-undefended country and overran it. His calculation was that the world wouldn't care overly much. If he realized his mistake upon hearing President George Bush's declaration "This will not stand," he never admitted such.

Saddam, at war's end, stood at the head of a crippled citizenry, naked at last to the wider world as a bloodthirsty tyrant. He could claim descent from Muhammad and thus a pipeline to Allah; he could have a thousand statues erected, a thousand murals painted; he could dispose of traitors on charges trumped up or real (in the latter category, two sons-in-law who defected in 1995, then returned to Iraq, naively believing that Saddam would show forgiveness); he could cover up the monstrosities of his sadistic older son, Uday; he

**The Godfather (in bulletproof, Kevlar-lined hat): Good with a gun, he hunted game, and meted out execution personally. When Bill Clinton defeated Bush père, Saddam fired off a round in celebration.**

could expose his milder son, Qusay, to invidious Baghdadi prisons in an effort to toughen him up; he could host terrorists; he could align himself with what he called Palestine's righteous crusade against Israel; he could gas 5,000 Kurds; he could talk of America's lack of "a civilization, in the deep and comprehensive sense we give to civilization"—he could do all this, but it would no longer alter or forestall reality. He was a man on the brink. And his past was catching up to him.

# The First Gulf War

Iraq's invasion of Kuwait spurred a large international coalition to confront Saddam's territorial ambitions.

The night sky over Baghdad is riddled with tracer fire as the U.S.-led coalition carries out one of many sorties. Early on, air control was secured as cruise missiles and bombs pummeled command centers, bases and missile launchers.

Three months after Iraq's invasion of Kuwait, the Army's 1st Cavalry Division deploys across the Saudi desert as part of Operation Desert Shield. Despite the showy high-tech aspects of the war, there would be still the need for that eternal warrior, the foot soldier.

**B**y 1990, Saddam Hussein had, in essence, been running Iraq for 15 years. And yet, within his country he had few allies he could count on; outside its borders, fewer still. That July he stunned, angered and frightened many of his Arab brethren when he accused his tiny neighbor Kuwait of stealing oil from the Ramallah oil fields. The tyrant also excoriated Persian Gulf states for courting Western nations by depressing the price of petroleum, thereby making it tougher for his country to recover from the deep financial losses suffered in its war with Iran. Egypt's Hosni Mubarak and others tried to defuse the situation, but there really was no chance of that. For Saddam, the steadfast devotee of Nasser, this was the time to ascend to his rightful position. As leader of a powerful, unified Arab world, Saddam would show the West where resides the wisdom, and fury, of the ages.

On August 2, Saddam defiantly invaded Kuwait, calling it Iraq's 19th province. Reaction was swift. Saudi Arabia's King Fahd petitioned Washington and the U.N. for protection from the madman, and in response, President George Bush deployed Operation Desert Shield to defend Saudi lands. Within days, the Arab League voted to send troops to assist the U.S. effort.

Throughout the rest of the year, pressure mounted to oust Iraq from Kuwait. At the same time, protests in America heated up with the rallying cry, "No blood for oil." Congress authorized the President to use force to evict the Iraqis, and the day after a January 15, 1991, U.N. deadline passed, Bush pulled the trigger on the most devastating strategic air assault in history: Operation Desert Storm. Because the timing of the attack was as formalized as an invitation, all of America went home after work and watched from their living rooms as their TVs relayed and replayed spectacular, multihued images of bombs and missiles doing their business.

This was, however, a real event, and in the end, Iraqi fatalities were estimated at 100,000, with 300,000 wounded, 60,000 captured and 150,000 desertions. Early in the conflict, Saddam had termed it a holy war, and prophesied that in this "mother of all battles," Americans would drown in "pools of their own blood." Ground fighting was indeed intense, but brief, as America and its allies overwhelmed the Iraqis. In the war's final two days, the largest tank battle since World War II was waged. Two hundred Iraqi tanks were destroyed; the Coalition lost not one. In all, 147 Americans were killed in the 42-day action, 159 were lost in nonhostile actions, and the wounded numbered 467.

As threatened, Saddam fired Scud missiles at Israel, but to little effect. The Israelis, at the urging of the U.S., did not retaliate, and the Western-Arab partnership survived. Saddam committed his typical dastardly deeds—mistreating prisoners, poisoning the environment—but he was finally made to stop.

And yet, he had survived Gulf War I. What would that mean?

With the battle for the air won, Secretary of Defense Richard Cheney visits U.S. headquarters in Saudi Arabia to discuss the forthcoming ground war with the Chairman of the Joint Chiefs of Staff, Gen. Colin Powell, and Desert Storm chief Gen. Norman Schwarzkopf. Below, Cpl. Scott Slabaugh awaits transport from Saudi Arabia to Iraq. At right, with dense smoke rising from oil-well fires set by retreating Iraqi soldiers, Marines patrol in a humvee.

In the aftermath, the roughnecks of a Canadian firm, Safety Boss, gained a solid reputation fighting oil fires in Kuwait; in just 200 days they capped 180 wells. (Canada was an ally in the war.) Above, President Bush, a former Navy combat pilot, tosses souvenir tie clips to U.S. forces gathered in Saudi Arabia. At right, on March 10, 1991, Staff Sgt. Daniel Stamaris, a former POW, receives a hero's welcome at Andrews Air Force Base in Maryland.

# TO THE BRINK OF WAR
# Drumbeat

Operation Desert Storm had been a masterpiece of military planning—sudden, electrifying thrusts in a convincingly one-sided action. But at the end, there was one dispiriting reality: Saddam Hussein had escaped his executioners and was free once more to feed his personal and territorial appetites. Heedless of the tremendous powers that sought to dethrone him, he would operate yet again with a defiant impunity, as the United Nations, United States and United Kingdom pressed over and over to make the tyrant acquiesce.

**March 1991** After Gulf War I, **Kurds, right,** and Shiites flee from Saddam's wrath. Press Secretary Marlin Fitzwater, responding to Saddam's attacks on the groups, declares: "We do not intend to involve ourselves in the internal power struggles of the country."

**April 1991** The U.S., U.K. and France initiate a "no fly" zone over northern Iraq to protect the Kurds. A similar zone is established in the south in 1992. These zones lead to cat-and-mouse dramas with Iraqis locking onto allied planes. They shoot at them hoping, in the jargon of American pilots, they will fire a "golden B.B." that will down a U.S. craft. The American response is to pulverize Iraqi air defenses.

**August 2, 1991** Iraq celebrates the first anniversary of its invasion of Kuwait. A giant scowling mosaic **doormat of George Bush, left,** bearing the inscription BUSH IS CRIMINAL, is laid at the

entry to Baghdad's Al-Rashid Hotel. Iraq calls the invasion a "stupendous victory."

**August 15, 1991** Five months after the cease-fire, the U.N. presses Iraq to comply with the terms of disarmament. During the next 12 years, 11 such resolutions would follow.

**April 1993** Bush makes a triumphant **visit to Kuwait, right.** The day before he arrives, officials arrest 14 suspected assassins. Once the U.S. verifies that Iraq has been involved, President Bill Clinton retaliates in June by launching a strike of 23 Tomahawk cruise missiles at the Iraqi intelligence headquarters in Baghdad.

Left: Coksun Aral/Sipa; Rabih Moghrabi/AP

**August 8, 1995** A caravan of Mercedes and Range Rovers streaks across the Iraqi desert toward Jordan. The man in charge of Iraq's weapons of mass destruction, **Hussein Kamel, above,** Saddam's son-in-law, is defecting with his brother, their wives (both daughters of Saddam) and a trove of state secrets. His rival, Uday, Saddam's wild-eyed son, follows in hot pursuit. Kamel's info proves revelatory. After Saddam tells him all is forgiven, he has Kamel killed.

**April 14, 1995** Facing criticism that sanctions are leading to starvation in Iraq, the U.N. launches an oil-for-food program to direct the country's funds to food and medicine rather than Saddam's military plans and lavish lifestyle. Iraq doesn't approve the program until May 1996, and the first food does not reach Iraqis till March 1997.

**July 1995** Iraq demands that the U.N. end inspections and sanctions by August 31. The demand meets with some sympathy, especially in France and Russia, which are eager to resume business with Iraq. The weapons-inspection team hints that its work is nearly done.

Al Siyassah/Sipa

**June 25, 1996** A 5,000-pound truck bomb explodes at the **Khobar Towers, above,** in Saudi Arabia, where U.S. troops enforcing Iraq's southern no-fly zone are based. The blast kills 19 Americans and wounds 372. Saddam says that the U.S. "should send more coffins to Saudi Arabia because no one can guess what the future has in store." The attack is later linked to Iran.

**September 3, 1996** The U.S. launches Operation Desert Strike to drive Saddam from Kurdish territories. The U.S. also extends the southern no-fly zone from the 32nd to the 33rd parallel— essentially the Baghdad city limits.

**March 26, 1997** Secretary of State Madeleine Albright says that the United States hopes to work with a "successor regime" in Baghdad.

**November 26, 1997** Saddam declares that his presidential compounds are off-limits to inspectors.

**January 26, 1998** A newly formed group of very powerful yet out-of-power conservatives, the Project for the New American Century, advocates changing American policy on Iraq. The group, which includes Donald Rumsfeld, Richard Perle and Paul Wolfowitz, tells Clinton that sanctions and containment have not worked. PNAC advocates "the removal of Saddam Hussein's regime from power."

**February 20, 1998** United Nations Secretary-General Kofi Annan brokers an end to the crisis by doubling the oil-for-food program to $10.5 billion a year, roughly Iraq's oil revenues before the Gulf War. In exchange, Saddam agrees to cooperate with inspectors.

**August 1998** Scott Ritter, a former Marine hired to beef up U.N. inspections, quits. He has complained that U.S., U.K. and Israeli intelligence agencies are withholding facts. He calls U.N. Special Commission (UNSCOM) inspections "a surrender to the Iraqi leadership."

**October 31, 1998** Clinton signs the Iraq Liberation Act, which will "support efforts to remove the regime headed by Saddam Hussein." The act sets aside $97 million in aid for opposition groups; most of it languishes unspent. That same day, Iraq stops cooperating with inspectors.

**November 14, 1998** To avert an air attack, Saddam promises compliance.

**December 15, 1998** Head weapons-inspector Richard Butler presents a devastating report to the U.N. He complains the Iraqis are still playing games, hiding equipment and not letting his team talk to key workers.

**December 16, 1998** The U.S. and U.K. bomb Iraq in Operation Desert Fox. The attack, on suspected chemical, biological and nuclear weapons plants, uses nearly as many missiles as were launched in the Gulf War. Republicans grouse that Clinton ordered the attack to distract from his pending impeachment resulting from his affair with Monica Lewinsky.

**December 19, 1998** Iraq vows that UNSCOM will never return. France proposes softening the embargo. The inspections end after eight years, during which UNSCOM finds and destroys 39,000 chemical munitions, 690 tons of chemical agents, 817 Scud missiles, and equipment and chemicals used to make the banned weapons.

**December 17, 1999** After a year of no inspections, a new weapons-inspection team is formed: the U.N. Monitoring, Verification and Inspection Commission (UNMOVIC). Swedish diplomat Hans Blix will later take the helm.

**January 10, 2001** The status of Lt. Comdr. Michael Speicher, a pilot shot down on the first day of the Gulf War, is changed from Killed in Action to Missing in Action. The U.S. had thought his F-18 Hornet exploded before he ejected. Iraqi defectors, however, report seeing him after the crash. Bush later cites the Speicher incident in his case against Iraq.

**January 2001** Experts say that a surge in Syrian oil sales means Saddam has opened a pipeline closed during the Iran-Iraq war, thereby flouting sanctions.

**February 22, 2001** One month into office, President George W. Bush orders the bombing of missile sites in Iraq, saying,

"The mission was . . . to send him a clear message that this administration will remain engaged in that part of the world. I think we accomplished that mission. We got his attention."

**September 11, 2001** Terrorists use three airplanes as missiles to destroy the **World Trade Center, below** (this mural was found in Iraq during Gulf War II), and damage the Pentagon. The plan for another plane to strike Washington, D.C., is foiled, and the craft crashes in Pennsylvania.

**September 12, 2001** Saddam says: "The United States reaps the thorns its rulers have planted in the world."

**September 24, 2001** *New York Times* conservative columnist William Safire links Iraq to al-Qaeda, citing Ansar Al Islam, a training camp in Kurdistan.

**October 5, 2001** Fear of biological and chemical terrorism spreads after photograph editor Robert Stephens dies when his employer, the *Sun,* receives anthrax-laced mail.

**October 7, 2001** Arab network Al Jazeera airs a video of **Osama bin Laden, top,** at a cave saying, "One million Iraqi children have thus far died in Iraq although they did not do anything wrong."

**October 26, 2001** In what may be the most direct link between Iraq and al-Qaeda, a Czech politician says that an Iraqi intelligence officer met with September 11 hijacker Mohammed Atta in Prague seven months earlier. The story is later doubted, but columnist Safire considers it a casus belli, saying the story has been discredited only by "U.S. spooks who may be covering up a missed signal from Prague about September 11."

**February 12, 2002** Secretary of State Colin Powell tells the Senate Budget Committee, "It has long been, for several years now, a policy of the United States government that a regime change would be in the best interest of the region [and] the best interest of the Iraqi people."

**March 2002** As part of a longtime campaign to align himself with the Palestinians, Saddam offers a $25,000 reward to the families of suicide bombers. This is 15 times more than the average Palestinian makes in a year.

**March 25, 2002** *The New Yorker* publishes a chilling story by Jeffrey Goldberg detailing Saddam's gas attack on the Kurdish village of Halabja in 1988.

The story reveals that it was a methodical killing experiment to establish the most effective ways to gas civilians.

**June 1, 2002** At **West Point, below,** Bush delivers the commencement address: "The war on terror will not be won on the defensive. We must take the battle to the enemy, disrupt his plans and confront the worst threats before they emerge."

**July 12, 2002** About 90 Iraqi military officers and defectors meet in London to discuss the overthrow of Saddam.

**August 1, 2002** Iraq invites Hans Blix to Baghdad, not for actual inspections but for "technical talks" of possible future inspections. He rejects the offer.

**August 15, 2002** Brent Scowcroft, former national security adviser to the President's father, writes in a *Wall Street Journal* column that war with Iraq would "put at risk our campaign against terrorism as well as stability and security in a vital region of the world."

**September 4, 2002** As the country returns from summer vacation, President Bush sets out to convince Congress, the American public and the world of the need to invade Iraq. He promises to get approval before he acts. "Today, the process starts," Bush says. "[Saddam] has sidestepped, crawfished, wheedled out of any agreement he had made not to harbor, not to develop weapons of mass destruction."

**September 7, 2002** White House Chief of Staff Andrew Card explains the timing of the war in *The New York Times:* "From a marketing point of view, you don't introduce new products in August."

**September 8, 2002** National Security Advisor Condoleezza Rice says the world may never know whether Saddam has weapons of mass destruction—until he uses them. "We don't want the smoking gun to be a mushroom cloud."

**September 10, 2002** British PM Tony Blair makes his case. "So let me tell you why I say Saddam Hussein is a threat that has to be dealt with. He has twice before started wars of aggression. Over one million people died in them . . . I sometimes think that there is a kind of word fatigue about chemical and biological weapons. We're not talking about some mild variants of everyday chemicals, but anthrax, sarin and mustard gas."

**September 11, 2002** On the first anniversary of the terrorist attacks, the House Armed Services Committee hears evidence that if Iraq were to get hold of nuclear material, it could build an atomic bomb in six months.

**September 12, 2002** President Bush tells the U.N. General Assembly that Iraq is a "grave and gathering danger" and says if they don't deal with Iraq, the U.S. will. "The Security Council resolutions will be enforced—the just demands of peace and security will be met—or action will be unavoidable," Bush says.

**September 25, 2002** Senate Majority Leader Tom Daschle lashes out at the administration for politicizing the war in time for congressional elections. The tirade is in response to Bush's remark that Democrats don't care about national security. Daschle points to a floppy disk found in a D.C. park that contained Bush strategist Karl Rove's private exhortation to Republicans to "focus on war" in their fall campaigns.

**September 27, 2002** At a fund-raiser for a Senate candidate, President Bush says of Saddam: "After all, this is the guy who tried to kill my dad."

**Fall 2002** Scott Ritter, the former Marine who quit the U.N. inspection team because it was too lax, returns to the scene as an antiwar voice. He says the inspections actually had worked and Saddam is no threat to the U.S.

**October 11, 2002** Congress authorizes war on Iraq. Five days later, **President Bush, right,** with senators John McCain and Joseph Lieberman, authorizes the use of force against Iraq.

**November 8, 2002** The U.N. Security Council unanimously approves Resolution 1441: Iraq must identify its nonconventional weapons and submit to inspections—including the palaces. The U.N. warns Iraq that if it fails to comply, it will "face serious consequences."

**November 18, 2002** The first United Nations inspectors arrive.

**December 4, 2002** The Pentagon announces that in several days there will be a call-up of 10,000 reservists; 50,000 troops are already in the Gulf region.

**December 7, 2002** Iraq hands over to the U.N. 12,000 pages of what it calls a complete and final disclosure of its weapons of mass destruction. This is the ninth time that the country has made a "full and complete" disclosure.

**January 9, 2003** In his first report, **Hans Blix, left,** says that in the course of the inspections, they have not found any "smoking gun," but notes that the Iraqis are not helping much.

**January 20, 2003** Rumsfeld tells *The New York Times* that the determination of whether Iraq is cooperating needs to be made "in weeks, not in months or years." This concept is soon adopted by the rest of the Coalition. By the end of the month, both Blair and Bush use the phrase, and two months to the day, war begins.

**January 21, 2003** Bush again warns Saddam that "time is running out . . . this looks like a rerun of a bad movie and I'm not interested in watching it."

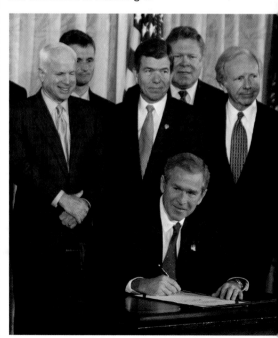

February 7, 2003 Acting on increased terrorist chatter, the Department of Homeland Security raises the national threat level from yellow ("elevated") to orange ("high"). Three days later, it advises buying duct tape and plastic sheeting to create a sealed room in case of a chemical attack.

February 14, 2003 As the U.S. and U.K. prepare to offer up a second resolution authorizing war on Iraq, the weapons inspectors report that Iraq has started to cooperate more.

February 15, 2003 A weekend of massive protests in **London, left,** and around the world decry the threat of war in Iraq.

February 28, 2003 Hans Blix gives another mixed report to the United Nations that pleases no one.

March 1, 2003 Turkey says no to an American request to base troops there. The U.S. had hoped to persuade Turkey with generous payments, thereby gaining access to a northern front.

March 5, 2003 France, Germany and Russia issue a joint statement saying they will not allow the U.N. to authorize

January 23, 2003 Rumsfeld irritates France and Germany by referring to them as Old Europe.

February 5, 2003 During a speech at the United Nations in which he presents the case for war, **Colin Powell, right,** displays a vial of powder that represents dry anthrax. Powell also plays audiotapes of Iraqi soldiers who are disposing of banned weapons before inspections.

One Iraqi officer says: "Stop talking about it. They are listening to us. Don't give any evidence that we have these horrible agents."

February 5, 2003 North Korea announces it has started an old nuclear reactor, prompting fears it could build an atomic arsenal while the U.S. is preoccupied with Iraq. Critics of an Iraqi war say North Korea is the real concern.

Sergio Barrenechea/EFE/Sipa

war on Iraq. A veto by any of the three could block the resolution.

**March 7, 2003** British Foreign Secretary Jack Straw proposes a final deadline for Iraqi compliance of March 17. French Foreign Minister Dominique de Villepin calls it a pretext for war.

**March 10, 2003** French President Jacques Chirac says, "Whatever happens, France will vote no."

**March 10, 2003** The U.S. asks for use of Turkey's airspace, while fearing that Turkey will enter Iraq to fight Kurds there.

**March 11, 2003** Rumsfeld says it is "unclear" if Britain, America's main partner, will join in the attack. The British call his remarks "curious."

**March 16, 2003** Main **Coalition leaders, above,** Blair, Spanish Prime Minister Jose Maria Aznar and Bush meet in the Azores

to discuss strategy. They give the U.N. one day to enforce its resolutions.

**March 17, 2003** Realizing they will be defeated, the U.S. and U.K. withdraw their second U.N. resolution without a vote. In a TV address, George Bush gives Saddam 48 hours to leave Iraq. Aides

call this the Get Out of Dodge speech. No one expects Saddam to leave; this is a warning to foreigners to flee.

**March 18, 2003** Saddam refuses offers of exile from other Arab leaders.

**March 19, 2003** War begins.

# Attack

Smoke over Baghdad—a familiar sight. Perhaps there were some who recalled 1958, while many others returned to 1991. In March 2003, smoke billows anew. Baghdad is aflame. War is on.

The western bank of the timeless Tigris River takes on a Goyaesque palette as Coalition forces pound their targets on March 21 in the first installment of "Shock and Awe." It is noteworthy that surrounding, nontargeted areas appear as they would on any evening.

Giles Penfound/AP

On March 20 in Kuwait, the U.S. 101st
Airborne receives orders. Above: Lt. Col.
Tim Collins of the Royal Irish Regiment
rallies his troops: "We go to liberate,
not to conquer. We will not fly our flags
in their country. We are entering Iraq to
free a people, and the only flag which
will be flown in that ancient land is
their own. Show respect . . . If there are
casualties of war then remember that
when they woke up and got dressed in
the morning they did not plan to die this
day. Allow them their dignity in death.
Bury them properly and mark their
graves . . . We will bring shame on
neither our uniform or our nation."

March 19 **Gulf Region** Aboard the
USS *Constellation,* Vice Adm. Timothy
Keating, in his address to the troops,
states, "You will contribute in a
magnificent way to the rewriting of
history." The ship's speakers then blast
Queen's anthem, "We Will Rock You."

March 19 **Gulf Region** Seventeen Iraqis
surrender to American troops before the
war has begun.

Jean-Marc Bouju/AP

On March 21, a teleconference between Washington, D.C., Tampa and Qatar involves many of the major players in the American war effort. Donald Rumsfeld (in sweater vest) chairs the session, with Chairman of the Joint Chiefs of Staff Richard Myers to his left. To Rumsfeld's right is Deputy Secretary of Defense Paul Wolfowitz. On the right half of the video screen, Gen. Tommy Franks speaks from Qatar, while on the left his deputy commander, Gen. Michael DeLong, weighs in from Tampa.

March 19 **United States** The American people ready for war as the President's 48-hour deadline expires tonight.

March 19 **Washington, 3 p.m.** CIA director George Tenet gets a tip on Saddam's exact location: a Baghdad bunker where he may be holed up for the night, possibly with both his sons. Tenet rushes to the White House.

March 19 **Washington, 4 p.m.** In the Oval Office, Bush and his top advisers— Tenet, Cheney, Powell, Rumsfeld, Rice, Card and Air Force General Myers, Chairman of the Joint Chiefs, consider the options. The plan had been for bombing to begin the next day, with the Coalition destroying Iraqi air defenses before other missions ensued. If the U.S. is to seize this opportunity, Gen. Tommy Franks tells the President, the bombers must leave Iraqi airspace under cover of darkness. Bush has until 7:15 to decide.

March 19 **Washington, 7:12 p.m.** "Let's go," says Bush, ordering the start of Operation Iraqi Freedom.

March 19 **Washington, 8 p.m.** The 48-hour deadline expires.

March 19 **Washington, 10:16 p.m.**
President Bush speaks to America: "My
fellow citizens, at this hour, American
and Coalition forces are in the early
stages of military operations to disarm
Iraq, to free its people and to defend the
world from grave danger . . . A campaign
on the harsh terrain of a nation as
large as California could be longer and
more difficult than some predict."

March 20 **Baghdad** Two F-117A stealth
fighters drop 2,000-pound bunker
busters on three Baghdad buildings,
which are also hit by 40 Tomahawk
cruise missiles. Workers frantically
crawl through the rubble. Some say
Saddam is dead; others that he was
carried away on a stretcher.

**A British Royal Marine (right) fires a
wire-guided missile at an Iraqi position
on the Al Faw peninsula on March 21.
Above: Two days later, the USS *Cape
St. George*, a guided-missile cruiser in
the eastern Mediterranean, launches
a Tomahawk Land Attack missile.**

Members of the U.S. 15th Marine Expeditionary Unit slake the thirst of this prisoner in southern Iraq on March 21. Just one hour after the unit crossed the border from Kuwait into Iraq, some 200 Iraqis surrendered. More than 7,000 were taken prisoner during the war, but the military worked toward trying to release people as soon as possible, to reduce friction as well as the burden. Right: Commandos from the British Royal Marines take a position as they fight their way through an Iraqi town

**March 20 Iraq, 8:30 a.m.**
A haggard-looking Saddam appears on Iraqi TV. Or does he? Some doubt that the man with puffy eyes and huge glasses looking down at a notebook is him. This is the first of several times that intelligence agencies try to verify Saddam sightings and what date they are from. Even his former mistress Parisoula Lampsos is questioned.

**March 20 Iraq Nine of**
Rumelia's 1,000 oil wells are torched. To avert an ecological disaster, 60,000 Coalition troops cross the border four hours ahead of schedule.

**March 20 Kuwait, 6:20 p.m.**
Air-raid sirens sound as Iraqi missiles land in Kuwait, where more than 100,000 Coalition troops are based. Soldiers and civilians rush to protect themselves from what they fear may be chemical weapons. Iraqi Information Minister Muhammad Said al-Sahhaf—who will become known as Baghdad Bob—denies they are the banned Scuds.

**March 21 Umm Qasr, 12:23 p.m.**
U.S. Marines raise the flag over this port city, then quickly lower it, hoping to quell any fears of an occupation. Soldiers and local citizens tear down images of Saddam.

**March 21 Iraq Turkey sends**
some 1,000 troops over the border, ignoring American requests. Ostensibly, Turkey wants to keep Kurdish refugees from flooding into its country

**March 21 Iraq** The Coalition suffers its first deaths. A U.S. Marine helicopter crashes, killing eight British and four Americans. The U.S. reveals that two other Marines have died, one in the Rumelia oil fields and one in Umm Qasr.

**March 21 Iraq, 9:45 p.m.** "Shock and Awe" begins in earnest. About 1,500 bombs strike Saddam's palaces and government buildings in Baghdad and the cities of Mosul, Kirkuk and Tikrit. Shock and Awe is calculated to be so devastating, so accurate, that Iraqis will simply give up. In Gulf War I, 10 percent of the bombs and missiles were precision-guided; technology has improved so that "smart bombs" will make up the vast majority of this campaign.

**March 21 Washington** Rumsfeld says of the Iraqis, "They're beginning to realize the regime is history. And as that realization sets in, their behavior is likely to begin to tip and change."

**March 21 New York, 4 p.m.** With the uncertainty of war removed and the battle well begun, the Dow rallies 8 percent in one week, the biggest such gain in 20 years.

The corpse of an Iraqi soldier lies wrapped in a blanket not far from the trench where he died during an assault on the Al Faw peninsula by Britain's 29 Commando Regiment Royal Artillery and the 40 Commando Royal Marines. This took place on March 22, the same day the U.K. suffered the tragic loss of two helicopters in a crash. With targets in the south as their goal, British troops see heavy action as the war unfolds.

**March 22 Iraq** As Coalition bombing continues, Iraqis set fire to oil in trenches surrounding potential targets. The intent is unclear. The smoke will interfere with laser-guided bombs, but it won't throw off the more numerous satellite-guided missiles. "Salam Pax," a Baghdad resident who has become a media star for his Web log of events, says (verbatim): "4:30p.m. (day 3) half an hour ago the oil filled trenches were put on fire. First watching Al-jazeera they said that these were the places that got hit by bombs . . . My cousine came and told me he saw police cars standing by one and setting it on fire."

**March 22 Iraq** Two British Sea Knight helicopters collide over the Persian Gulf, killing all seven on board, including an American.

**March 22 Iraq** Al Jazeera says more than 50 civilians have died and shows gruesome footage of mutilated children.

In Baghdad there was, of course, massive fear, anger and confusion—in some quarters, near panic. On Day Four of the conflict, even as Army Pfc. Jessica Lynch and other U.S. POWs were being taken in Nasiriya, a rumor spread in the Iraqi capital that an American pilot had been downed near the Tigris. Citizens (left) and soldiers (above) rush to the riverbank and beat the bushes. Near a smoke screen, gunfire was heard. It was from Iraqis shooting into the brush. No pilot was down, none was found.

**March 22 World** Antiwar protests dominate the weekend, with 100,000 marchers in New York City and 200,000 in London. There are antiwar rallies in every major European capital. In Yemen a violent peace demonstration ends with two dead. Protests also rage in Jakarta, Seoul and Bangkok.

**March 23** **Camp Pennsylvania, Kuwait, 1:21 a.m.** U.S. Army Sgt. Hasan Akbar, a Muslim convert who disapproved of the war, allegedly throws three grenades into officers' tents, then shoots at them as they flee. Two die in the incident.

**March 23** **Kuwait** A British Tornado fighter jet is shot down by a U.S. Patriot missile, killing two.

**March 23** **Nasiriya, Iraq** Before dawn, six vehicles from the 507th Maintenance Company get separated from the 3rd Infantry Division. Realizing its mistake, the convoy heads back to the Euphrates but two buses block the way and Iraqi tanks open fire. Some scramble free, but others are unaccounted for, including three women: Pfc. Jessica Lynch, Spc. Shoshana Johnson and Pfc. Lori Piestewa. Al Jazeera shows Iraqis gloating over four dead Americans, one in an extremely humiliating position.

**March 24** **Iraq** Saddam (or a double?) speaks on television and refers to some recent actions, dampening hopes that he had already been killed.

**March 24** **Nasiriya** Eight Marines die in ambushes at this key crossroad to Baghdad, which is now dubbed Ambush Alley. Soldiers say that guerrillas jumped out of taxis to shoot at them.

**This March 24 memorial service near Najaf, Iraq, is being held for Army Reserve Spc. Brandon Tobler, who was assigned to the 671st Engineer Brigade. The 19-year-old logistics specialist from Portland, Ore., was killed when his humvee crashed during a sandstorm. Before the war, he worked in a Best Buy electronics store near his home.**

# The World Reacts

The explosions in Iraq reverberated in streets from Sydney to San Francisco.

**T**his war could not have come as less of a surprise. Yet when it finally broke out, the world erupted. Predictably, governments that had tried to prevent the war condemned it. "This military action cannot be justified," said Russian President Vladimir Putin, and his sentiments were shared by Chinese, French and German heads of state. Leaders of nations involved in the Coalition remained stoic. In the middle, there was a poignant melancholy. "I strongly regret that military action was necessary," said Denmark's Prime Minister Anders Fogh Rasmussen, "but I think it was." Pope John Paul II, who had opposed the war as unjust, expressed "profound sorrow."

There was little equivocation in the streets. French protesters stoned a McDonald's and staged a sit-in at the Place de la Concorde. In Helsinki, demonstrators chanted "George Bush, CIA/How many kids did you kill today?" Greeks and Italians went on strike. In Indonesia, the world's most populous Islamic country, there were massive prayer rallies. Militant Muslims pledged to answer the call to *jihad.* Egyptian President Hosni Mubarak watched the passion rise and made a chilling prediction: "When it is over, if it is over, this war will

have horrible consequences. Instead of having one bin Laden, we will have 100 bin Ladens."

The American satirical magazine *The Onion* offered an alternate label for the military mission: Operation Piss Off the Planet.

At home, sentiments jingoistic, patriotic, angry or just plain silly were expressed. While "No blood for oil" was heard in demonstrations coast to coast, polls indicated that most Americans backed the war—or, at the very least, the men and women waging war. Yellow ribbons bloomed again across the land, this time symbolizing support for the troops. In Fieldsboro, N.J., a smattering of yellow grew to overwhelm the town after Mayor Edward "Buddy" Tyler, an opponent of the war, ordered ribbons removed because they violated a town ordinance that banned displays on public property. Elsewhere, restaurants served Freedom Fries in place of French, and French's Mustard felt compelled to issue a statement denying any French connection. Such attention-drawing actions trivialized what was happening here. Alongside the more considered expressions of support and dissent, they were revealed as shallow, inappropriate, inane. There was a war on, after all.

**On March 22, a day of global protest, a father and daughter in Seville, Spain — a member of the U.S.-led Coalition — plead for peace. On March 28 at Xavier University in Cincinnati, Courtney Henderson attends a Support the Troops rally.**

In Moscow's Red Square, members of Russia's National Bolshevik Party loudly denounce America, while in a city park in São Paulo, Brazil, women at a bridal clothing expo quietly spell out Paz—Peace. On March 20, one of the larger demonstrations in the United States took place in San Francisco where protesters blocked traffic in the financial district. Nearly 1,500 people are arrested, including this woman.

Oleg Nikishin/Getty

Rickey Rogers/Reuters

David Paul Morris/Getty

# TOM STODDART'S WAR

He got into photography 32 years ago, at the age of 17, when an editor in his native England told him the job offered "a champagne lifestyle on a beer salary." The least glamorous but most richly rewarding stops along the way for Stoddart have been at the Berlin Wall on the day it fell, in South Africa covering Nelson Mandela's election, and during a four-year stay in besieged Sarajevo. He recently spent two years building a photographic document of the AIDS scourge in Africa, which won him the prestigious World Understanding Award, given by the University of Missouri's School of Journalism. In the spring of 2003 he is supposed to receive this honor, but Stoddart is otherwise engaged: There is a war on. He arrives in Kuwait on March 12, and on the 13th is embedded with the 539 Assault Squadron of the Royal Marines, an elite group of 100 men who operate on water with their fast boats, landing craft and hovercraft. Stoddart is thrilled by his assignment because he realizes it will take him to the forefront of the action. The only photojournalist attached to the 539 unit, he spends a week getting to know the Marines, who continue to train as war looms. On the day that the Coalition attacks, Stoddart and members of the Assault Squadron make three approaches in hovercraft to set down on Al Faw peninsula beach in southern Iraq but can't as the terrain is too heavily mined. Stoddart and the men in the photograph at left move up through the marshes in a landing craft and, at this instant, are about to set foot in Iraq.

**" The men are suspicious of me at first. But some of them realize that I've seen more war than most of them have, and then things are better. As we approach the beach, there are obstacles and mines everywhere, it's reminiscent of D-Day. When we patrol the marshes, the men are alert and tense. The Marines have to clear this area, and they don't know what's out there. "**

When moving on the Khawr Az Zubayr waterway on March 30, one of the squadron's landing craft is blasted by an Iraqi rocket; one Marine is killed and others injured. Kevin Jones (above) is blown into the water, then is pulled into a hovercraft by another Marine and BBC cameraman Steve Gray (right). Shrapnel in Jones's thigh rests a quarter inch from his femoral artery: He is shivering, in shock, but alive. In the photo opposite, the 539's commanding officer, the heavily decorated Lt. Col. Nick Anthony, prepares to rally his men.

**The men have been fighting all night on a nighttime patrol. They've just been told one of their comrades has been killed. They're sitting by the waterway, exhaustion on their faces. The adrenaline is flooding, but tiredness and grief are overcoming them. It is a moment that shows . . . well, it shows just how awful war can be. It shows how awful war really is.**

In Basra on April 10, three days into the city's liberation, soldiers in the British Army's Black Watch Regiment distribute fresh water. Below: A man with prayer beads watches as a gas-processing plant burns in the Zubayr oil field. Right: five miles west of Basra.

As we reach Basra, I leave the 539 Squadron and start to move about. It's an astonishing and distressing scene. I am in a place where a huge amount of the oil in the region is harvested, and there is immense poverty and deprivation. Everything I see indicates just how hard it is going to be for Iraq to put things together in any kind of positive way after the war.

> **In the first days of the new Basra there is a lot of crime and a lot of joy. They used to call Saddam's yacht a floating palace. Now while some kids their age are off looting, dozens of other boys wait to take turns jumping off it into the river. It seems they're saying, 'One leap and we're free!'**

A boy carries a box he has stolen from the burned-out Sheraton; other looters kneel, hooded and cuffed, inside the grounds of Saddam Hussein's Basra palace, HQ for British forces. Saddam's bombed-out yacht is a site for frolic.

# A Free Press

## Reports from the front have been posted for ages. This war, however, provided a whole new look.

**O**f arms and the man I sing." So begins *The Aeneid,* an epic poem fashioned 2,000 years ago by Virgil, which in part chronicles the fate of the Roman armies. Four centuries earlier, Pericles eulogized the soldiers who had died at Marathon defending Greece from the Persians. In the Middle Ages, yet another conflict between the West and Arabian lands—the Crusades—was amply represented in the sagas of both participants. War is hell, and this is known even by those who have never heard the saber strike home, because there have always been others who would relay the grim or heroic details.

America's military history proves no exception.

The Civil War, the Rough Riders, doughboys and the flag on Suribachi—the details were recorded in word or photograph, and so we know the stories. Then, in the 1960s, technological advances gave birth to the first "TV war": Vietnam. It was not live television, of course. Footage had to be shipped out, and it was heavily edited. Still, memories of body bags on the nightly news help support the idea that the defeat in Southeast Asia was due, at least in part, to the media's provocation. That notion ensured that the military would not permit another Vietnam during Operation Desert Storm in 1991. There would be "overwhelming force" applied to the enemy—and to the press.

Cheryl Diaz Meyer/Dallas Morning News/Corbis

**Cheryl Diaz Meyer of *The Dallas Morning News* transmits her photos on March 21 by satellite phone. She is with the 2nd Marine Tank Battalion, southwest of Basra.**

Few journalists ever got close to the fighting.

Criticism of the Pentagon's media control in Gulf War I, which was exacerbated during the Afghanistan campaign of 2002 when reporters were herded into a windowless building in Kandahar so they wouldn't see injured U.S. soldiers, was carefully weighed by military authorities as they planned Gulf II. Then it was announced: Journalists would be assigned to frontline troops who would actually be fighting the war.

The change of heart by the Pentagon was not so much a sudden infatuation with a free press as an advance strike in the war for the public's hearts and minds. "Having an independent, objective reporter on the battlefield has the effect of mitigating disinformation," explained Pentagon spokesman Bryan Whitman. "Saddam Hussein is a practiced liar. I can't think of a better way to counter that fact."

The Pentagon took on the task of media relations with the same attention to detail employed in the prosecution of the war itself, hiring savvy media consultants to polish up some of the rusty old soldiers. Hundreds of news organizations

**This photographer for London's *Sunday Telegraph* and a woman from a Dutch TV network take cover from artillery fire. They're traveling with Kurdish volunteer fighters.**

applied to be part of the "embed" program, and the Pentagon eventually approved 250 of them. The list included ABC, Al Jazeera (from Qatar), *The Albuquerque Tribune, The Chicago Tribune, The Chosun Ilbo* (from South Korea), *Inside Edition,* ITAR-TASS News Agency of Russia, *Le Monde* (from France), *People, Rolling Stone* and Xinhua News Agency (from China). The military ran a media "boot camp," where journalists went through tactical training, learned first aid, and, finally, took a five-mile march. GOV'T PREPS NEWSIES FOR WAR EFFORT, headlined *Variety.*

The technology of journalism had changed since U.S. newsies last launched a war effort, and this assured that coverage of Gulf War II would be of an entirely new kind. Satellite dishes, which allowed phone conversations from just about anywhere, weighed 140 pounds instead of a thousand; the new dish could be set up in 20 minutes instead of five hours. Though transmission speeds remained sluggish, making audio reports jerky and images grainy, they were good enough to allow live television dispatches from the middle of nowhere (which was, because of "operational security" rules, about as specific as a reporter could be). For NBC, David Bloom refined the new

equipment even further. He worked with the military to customize an M-88 tank recovery vehicle with a digital camera, sat-phone and microwave dish that sent a signal to a transmitter mounted on a gyroscope in a pickup truck, the "Bloommobile," which followed up to five miles behind.

Amid the thousands of journalists and support staff covering the war, some 600 were embedded with combat troops. This took a little getting used to for everyone. "We seem to see a line of vehicles off to the left there," reported a CBS embeddee

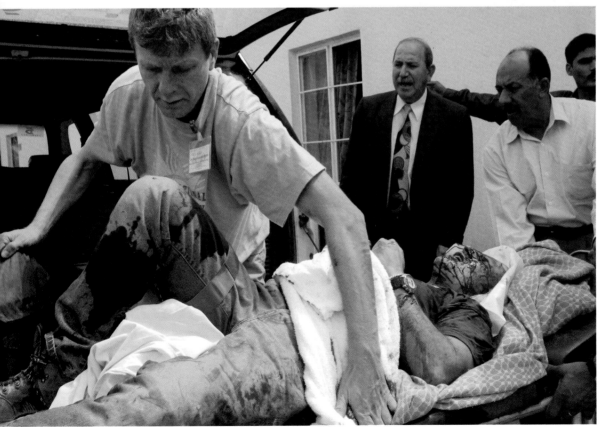

**The Palestine Hotel served as HQ for the press. Photographer Molly Bingham (top) was abducted there and later released. On April 8, U.S. gunfire hit the hotel, killing two. Reuters' Paul Pasquale (left) was wounded.**

Jobard/Sipa

who was on the move with the 1st Marine Division in southern Iraq. "Oh, sorry. It's a line of camels."

There were, of course, rules for the embedded journalists: They could not use their own vehicles, could not reveal locations of their units, could not broadcast live action without the permission of the commanding officer and could not in any way jeopardize operational security. But for the most part, they were free to show and describe what they saw. While doubters like Bernard Shaw, a former CNN star, worried that these embedded journalists would "become hostages of the military," it didn't seem to play out that way.

Reports of the many Iraqi casualties and those of the Coalition were what would be expected during wartime. But then one day during a firefight in northern Iraq, a U.S. soldier trying to elude enemy fire flipped his humvee into a ditch, killing himself and his passenger, embedded reporter Michael Kelly. He was the first American journalist to die, and two days later, NBC's Bloom, only 39 and the father of three, suffered a pulmonary embolism. "Report: Initial," a soldier said into his phone. "Enemy involvement: None. Name: Bloom, David. Military unit: Civilian. Status: Deceased." Bloom was known to be indefatigable, and when doctors told him to seek medical attention for

**Answering criticism of the hotel incident, Colin Powell said on April 21, "Our review . . . indicates that the use of force was justified and the amount of force was proportionate to the threat against United States forces."**

**Here looking every inch the international journalist, Peter Arnett said the wrong things to the wrong people at the wrong time. NBC and *National Geographic* cut the native New Zealander loose.**

cramps he was feeling behind his left knee, he ignored them. War, it turned out, was as dangerous as could be imagined, and risky in unpredictable ways.

British journalist Ciar Byrne called the war in Iraq "the worst ever for journalists," and facts supported the assessment. During the entire Vietnam War, for instance, 63 journalists were killed, which was about one tenth of one percent of the roughly 58,000 American military dead. In Gulf War II, 14 journalists died, a number equal to 10 percent of the 138 U.S. military fatalities.

There were other "casualties," as journalistic standards sometimes lost out to ambition, expe-

dience or plain greed. An L.A. *Times* photographer was sacked for sending his bosses a composite picture—without mentioning that it had been doctored. A Fox News engineer was arrested at Dulles International Airport while trying to bring in war "souvenirs": stolen paintings and other items. And Eason Jordan, CNN's chief news executive, caused a stir by unburdening himself, in a *New York Times* op-ed piece, of secrets about the Iraqi regime's brutality that he hadn't divulged at the time because, he said, to do so—to report the news—might have jeopardized CNN employees.

On the second Sunday of the war, Fox's Geraldo Rivera, who was traveling with an Army unit

Top: Michael Macor/San Francisco Chronicle/Corbis Saba; Fox News

**After a dispatch from Oliver North (top), Fox News said that he was "a military contributor . . . He is neither a reporter nor a correspondent." Right, the network's Geraldo Rivera stirs up a firestorm.**

but was not an embedded journalist, drew lines and circles in the sand to guide his viewers. By indicating his location he had clearly breached operational security, said Central Command, which had earlier sent a reporter for the *Christian Science Monitor* packing for a similar infraction.

Then there was the case of Peter Arnett. The only major television correspondent allowed to remain in Baghdad during the first Gulf War, Arnett, now 68, found himself in nearly the same position as Gulf II was heating up. The American television networks had pulled staff reporters out of Baghdad—or, as in the cases of Fox and CNN, had been booted out for what the Iraqi regime considered biased reporting. Once again, Arnett was feeding "exclusives" to the world from the heart of the enemy capital, this time for *National Geographic Explorer* and NBC. He even snagged an interview with Iraq's prime minister, Tariq Aziz. But when he gave an interview to Iraqi TV, on the same Sunday that Geraldo was drawing lines in the sand, Arnett crossed a line himself when he said, "The first war plan has failed because of Iraqi resistance." He also offered that his reporting about Iraqi civilian casualties "helps those who oppose the war." Arnett's words, voiced on Iraq's own network, were widely considered traitorous. At first, NBC defended him. But on Monday morning, *Today*'s Matt Lauer read a statement announc-

ing Arnett's termination.

An obvious benefit of having so many journalists in so many places, from the Pentagon's perspective and indeed that of many U.S. viewers, was to take away from "the enemy" whatever propaganda advantage it might have gained from portraying the war the way it wanted the war portrayed. Thus, while the unquenchably one-sided Information Minister Muhammad Said al-Sahhaf, a.k.a. Baghdad Bob, was shown at one of his press conferences saying that Coalition forces were not in Baghdad, Fox News was showing, in split screen, reporter Greg Kelly riding a tank through

Bottom: NBC News/AP; Reuters/Corbis

**LIVE**

**DAVID BLOOM**
WITH THE THIRD INFANTRY DIVISION
IN IRAQ
NOW ON MSNBC.COM: U.S. STEPS UP

**Not far from the Euphrates River, Army soldiers desperately try to save the dying Bloom. The NBC reporter was known for his ardor.**

the city. Such arresting video moments were perhaps too few—a study by the Project for Excellence in Journalism found that 80 percent of TV stories by embeds featured reporters alone, giving reports—but they created lasting impressions.

What was the final score on embedding? NPR's John Burnett called it "an unnatural way to practice journalism," adding that "we need to have our own transportation to be independent." For Jim Axelrod of CBS, "There was some initial mistrust and suspicion: 'Who are you guys and what are

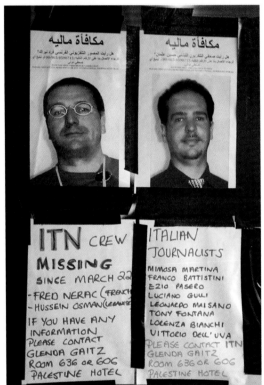

Top: ABC News/AP; Seamus Conlan/World Picture News

you gonna do to harm us?' But we got great stories and they got very positive coverage." His opinion comes close to confirming a criticism raised by many: that journalists developed a bias as they befriended soldiers. Countered CBS News chief Andrew Heyward, "You're not going to find a lot of Americans rooting for Iraq. That doesn't mean they're not objective and fair in their reporting."

So, this time, there were two armies at work in Iraq: one, the men and women in uniform; and then the writers, talkers, camera operators, pho-

tographers, technicians and translators. This latter unit delivered to the world the first 24/7 war. All day, all night, the action was reported by thousands, and watched by millions. That, finally, was the very substantial benefit of the Pentagon's decision. When something happened—a statue toppling—we were there. When something bad happened—a van full of Iraqi women and children shot apart at a checkpoint—the story moved instantly. The war was made real, in real time, and it was riveting.

**Michael Kelly (top), 46, talks on *Nightline* weeks before his death. These posters from the Palestine Hotel make all too clear the dangers faced by the press.**

# On the Ground

The forces that had been amassed in Kuwait headed for Baghdad, grappling with vicious sandstorms and other unwanted surprises.

Neither the halls of Montezuma nor the shores of Tripoli, this is the "road" to Baghdad. And, once more, these are the U.S. Marines—3rd Battalion, 4th Regiment—fighting a battle for their country.

Having donned protective suits, these soldiers from 2nd Battalion, 70 Armor are conducting a chemical test during an alert that proves false. They were also hit by a monster sandstorm, with winds approaching 100 mph, that has whipped up sand from as far away as Egypt and Libya. The storm severely hampered reinforcement and supply lines, which reached back to Kuwait. Long-range bombing continued, but two planes that had taken off from the carrier *Kitty Hawk* were forced to divert to Kuwait.

**March 25 Iraq** As a sandstorm of historic proportions engulfs Iraq, Americans face fierce opposition in Najaf.

**March 26 Northern Iraq** Since Turkey would not allow the U.S. to marshal an offensive from its territory, the only way to get troops into the north is to drop them in—which begins today as 1,000 troops of the 173rd Airborne Brigade parachute in and take control of a key airfield. It is the first major deployment north of Baghdad. In the days ahead, the soldiers organize with Kurdish allies to try to mount a northern front.

**March 26 Iraq** A convoy of Republican Guard vehicles reportedly racing south to shore up defenses in Karbala mysteriously disappears. U.S. officials later say it never existed.

Although the sandstorm provided cover for some advancing American troops, most were forced to dig in and wait it out. These soldiers from the Army's 3rd Infantry Division make the best of it at a captured airfield in southern Iraq. The conditions were tough enough, but after the sunset turned everything orange, the sky and all else then turned a deep, dark red, which had an unsettling effect on some of the troops.

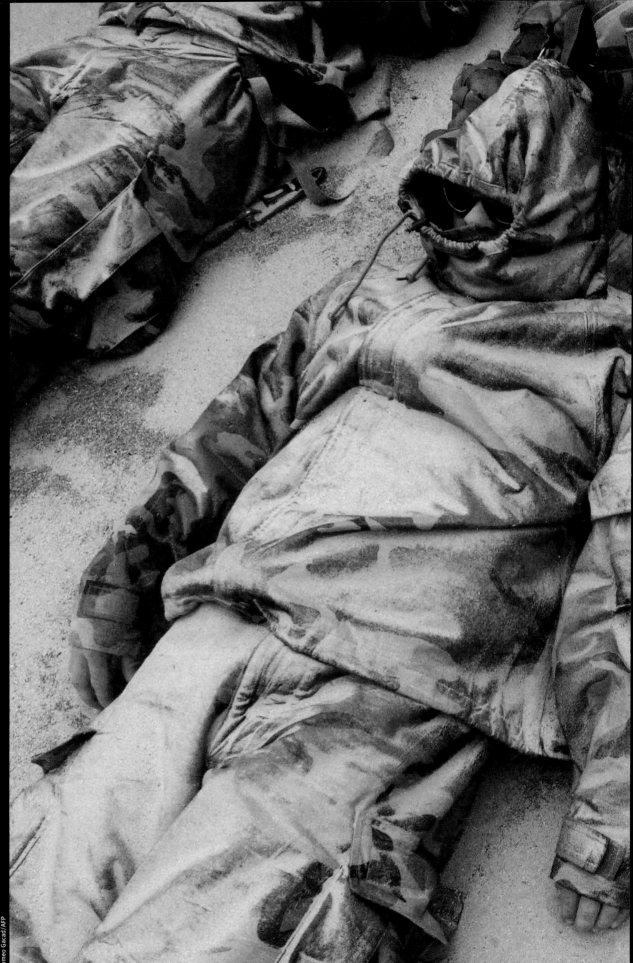

Brant Sanderlin/Atlanta Journal-Constitution

On March 26 in a village south of Basra, a British army medic sees to a four-day-old infant named Fahed who was born during the war (left). Above: An Iraqi man tries to kiss the cheek of an American Marine as the man pleads with the troops not to fire on a building. (The Marines thought there was a sniper on the roof.) Right: Army Sgt. Mark Strunk treats an Iraqi soldier.

Heading toward Baghdad, a U.S. Marine strides past a dead Iraqi soldier on a path running beside a road outside Nasiriya. The soldier was killed in a firefight with Marines when Iraqi forces unleashed an ambush from trenches along the road on March 26.

March 27 **Iraq The commander of the Army in the Persian Gulf, Lt. Gen. William Wallace, worries that war will drag on: "The enemy we're fighting is a bit different than the one we war-gamed against, because of these paramilitary forces." Among the war games used to prepare for real fighting was one that, at the time, (Ret.) Lt. Gen. Paul Van Riper said was too scripted. When Van Riper used motorcycle messengers or suicide speedboat bombers, his superiors simply nixed such moves and called a do-over.**

March 27 **The Pentagon announces it will send as many as 120,000 more troops to Iraq.**

On March 26, the
morning after the
terrible sandstorm,
nature provided yet
another twist when
the skies opened up
and turned the
countryside into a
vast mud pit. These
Marines from the 2nd
Battalion, 8th Marine,
are awakening in
Nasiriya after
spending the night
fighting the relentless
sand—only to end up
drenched. Once again,
vehicles are stranded
and the pace of the
war has slowed,
although there is
heavy fighting along
the Euphrates River.

An Iraqi raises his hands while others remain seated on a road in central Iraq near Qal'at Sukkar on March 27. A U.S. Marine keeps his weapon trained on the group. Iraqi irregulars in nonuniformed units have been a thorn in the side of advancing Marines, forcing them into urban areas they had hoped to avoid.

Damir Sagolj/Reuters

On March 27, the three children at right are scurrying to get to a food-distribution point in Zubayr, south of Basra in southern Iraq. Above, two days later, British soldiers have their hands full keeping order while they give out relief packages. Shortly before, the first British supply ship laden with aid, the *Sir Galahad*, had arrived in Umm Qasr. Many cities had been without aid for a week.

**March 27 Baghdad** The city undergoes the fiercest bombardment since the previous week's Shock and Awe campaign. The Information Ministry and Saddam's al-Salam palace are hit.

**March 28 Basra** Iraqi soldiers fire on their own countrymen, desperate civilians trying to flee the besieged city

**March 28 Washington** Donald Rumsfeld threatens Syria for sending night-vision goggles to Iraq. "We consider such trafficking as hostile acts."

**March 28 Washington** President Bush finds questions about the war getting bogged down "silly," a White House official tells reporters.

**March 29 World** For the second weekend in a row, massive antiwar protests are staged around the globe. Tens of thousands gather in London, Paris, Berlin, Rome, Barcelona, Cape Town, Kuala Lumpur, Melbourne . . . But the large French antiwar movement suffers a rift as anti-Semitism and anger at Israel become part of the dialogue

March 29 **Najaf** An Iraqi army officer dressed as a taxi driver feigns car trouble. When U.S. troops stop to help, a bomb kills four soldiers. Iraqi TV praises the suicide bomber as a "national hero."

March 29 **Northern Iraq** Kurds help U.S. Special Forces destroy the training camp of Ansar Al Islam, a terrorist group linked to al-Qaeda.

March 29 **Basra** A meeting hall where 200 Saddam loyalists are gathered is bombed.

March 29 **Nasiriya** Marines find the bodies of four missing U.S. servicemen, seized in an ambush a week earlier, in a shallow grave. Execution of prisoners, a war crime, is suspected.

March 31 **Iraq** Coalition forces move to within 50 miles of Baghdad.

March 31 **Kuwait** An Egyptian plows his truck into a line of U.S. soldiers outside a store at Camp Udairi, injuring 13 of the GIs.

Jerome Delay/AP

**Above:** Female relatives of Muhammad Jaber Hassan mourn beside his coffin at the Muhammad Sakran cemetery, outside of Baghdad, on Saturday, March 29. The 22-year-old man was killed when a bomb struck a market in the capital city. Of the 52 people who died in the explosion, at least 15 were interred along with Hassan. At right, on the same day, a Marine medic near Rifa, in eastern Iraq, cradles a four-year-old girl. Her mother was killed in a frontline cross fire, U.S. officers said.

Damir Sagolj/Reuters

This little girl will long remember that war is a nightmare. She is with many groups of families hastening to get out of Basra, Iraq's second-largest city; Saddam Hussein's troops are still inside the town, which is now surrounded by British forces. Saddam publicized photos of wounded children, blaming Coalition forces for their plight. His minions reportedly made threats against children as a means of getting their parents to fight in the war.

Dan Chung/AP

There were many reports of Coalition fighters being fired on by seemingly innocent civilians. Here, these American soldiers from A Company, 3rd Battalion, 7th Infantry Regiment warily approach a woman on a bridge over the Euphrates in the town of Hindiyah on March 31. She turned out to be wounded, and the soldier nearest her, 32-year-old Capt. Chris Carter, provided cover as medics took her away. The handsome Carter became something of the wit of the war. While the brass pondered the state of affairs in Baghdad, Carter had the answer: "I do believe this city is freakin' ours."

John Moore/AP

As the second week of the war was nearing its close, Coalition forces streaming from the south were making better headway, while efforts to mount any kind of northern offensive were proving difficult for Americans who had parachuted in. The air assault of Baghdad continued ceaselessly. On March 31, a day when U.S. bombs will hit the Old Presidential Palace, this Baghdadi offers a salute and a tear at the funeral of a victim of an earlier attack. There is intense fighting on this day in the cities and towns around Baghdad, and It mostly goes the Coalition's way. The heat is on.

March 31 **Iraq** Baghdad says that 4,000 volunteers from across the Arab world have heeded the call to *jihad* and will offer themselves to Allah as suicide bombers, their martyrdoms directed against American and British forces.

March 31 **Najaf** Soldiers, perhaps made jittery by the suicide bombing here two days earlier, and reports of more to come, open fire on a van that ignored warnings to stop at a checkpoint. It turns out the vehicle is filled with 13 women and children. Seven are killed and two wounded.

March 31 **Iraq** As if in answer to Donald Rumsfeld's questions of the previous day—"Where is Saddam Hussein? Where is Qusay, where is Uday, his sons?"—Iraqi TV broadcasts a videotape of Saddam in uniform, seated at a table, with his aides on his right and his sons on his left. It is not clear when the tape was made. Officials at the Pentagon say there are indications that Saddam's relatives are trying to flee Iraq.

# DAVID TURNLEY'S WAR

O ver 20 years, the Pulitzer Prize–winning photojournalist has gained access to war zones from Somalia and Rwanda to Bosnia and Chechnya. He has documented violence in Israel's West Bank and Beijing's Tiananmen Square—and, indeed, in Iraq during the first Gulf War. Now, in early March 2003, he is maneuvering along the northern Iraq border, trying to arrange to be smuggled into the country from Turkey. He makes contacts, gets to know the people, makes their pictures—including this one, of a Kurdish woman and her child returning home after the mother has finished her day's work in the fields. A plan is established to get Turnley and three others into Iraq, but it comes apart at the last moment. The Kurdish peshmergas agree to try again two days later, and in a raging downpour they lead Turnley and the others over hills and through ravines toward the Tigris River. There, they hide in the brush from Turkish soldiers in watchtowers, then pile into a small dinghy and cross the swollen river into Syria. They spend the first of four nights at a safe house. Turnley sleeps fitfully and awakens at 5:30. He'll be working in Iraq for CNN, so he calls headquarters in Atlanta. He learns the war began during the night. Now he's desperate to get into Iraq, and finally, after another dinghy trip across the Tigris in the dead of night, he does. Turnley is in the war zone again—familiar territory—and he quickly goes to work.

**❝ The night before we set off for northern Iraq, our peshmerga friends come to smoke more cigarettes and drink more tea with us at the safe house. The three men are in their 30s and 40s. Two of them have 10 children each. They are tough, tough men. The war has just started, and the way they tell it is, 'America, England, Iraq—boom, boom.' ❞**

Corbis

Bottom: On the eve of war, life goes on in Kurdistan, where men and women dance at a wedding. In his first week in Iraq, Turnley makes his way to Kifri near the Iranian border. Below: an elderly citizen in Kifri. Right: A Kurdish soldier patrols the market there.

“ We stop beside the road, 30 kilometers from Kifri. The Mahmud Ahmed Abdullah family, 74 strong, live in a field there, in tents made of sacking and sticks. They've left Kifri because they're afraid of missile attacks; the front line is only two miles from town. They say Iraqis fight only because Saddam hangs insubordinates. The family is for a free Kurdistan after Saddam. ”

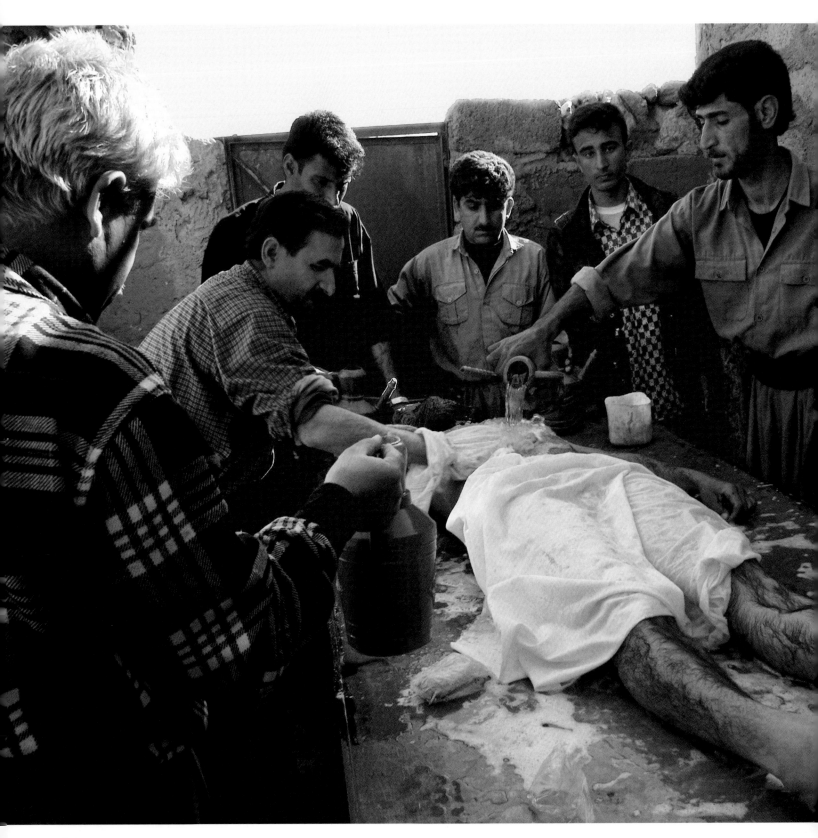

   **❝ We come upon a dramatic scene. Men, in the Muslim tradition, are behind a curtain in the backyard, washing the body and preparing it to be wrapped in a white sheet. Across the yard, three generations of women weep and shout, 'Saddam Hussein!' I haven't been amid such suffering in a long time, though it feels familiar—an echo of other wars I've covered. ❞**

April 1 is a day of mourning in Kifri, as a 26-year-old teacher
has been killed by an Iraqi mortar attack. Young men prepare
the body for burial and then carry the casket out while an
old woman grieves. Below: Women wail and beat their chests.

In the third week of the war, Turnley, moving south as the Iraqi defenses fall, reaches Baghdad. American tanks roll through the Old City, and women return home after seeking refuge during the Coalition bombing campaign. Explosions give way to music.

"I had been here in '91, before and after the war, and again in '96. I immediately sense that the mood has changed. After a 12-year embargo and now another war, Baghdadis seem drained of their life force. There's a look of real concern on their faces. People come up to me: 'Tell George Bush we are waiting—for a new government, food to eat, a return to order.'"

# Faces of the War

There is a danger, in an era when smart bombs are delivered from great distances, that war can seem depersonalized, no more real than a computer game. Should this happen, as it did to a large extent during the first Gulf War, then the horrors of war get lost, as do those moments when the very best in humanity shines through. In Gulf War II, images like the photo of a U.S. Marine cradling a motherless girl, or stories such as that of Marine Lance Cpl. Jose Gutierrez, who died for his new country although he was an "illegal alien" from Guatemala, brought war home to any who were paying attention. Three cases in particular—two involving dramatic rescues of prisoners of war, a third concerning a terribly injured Iraqi boy—touched the hearts of millions.

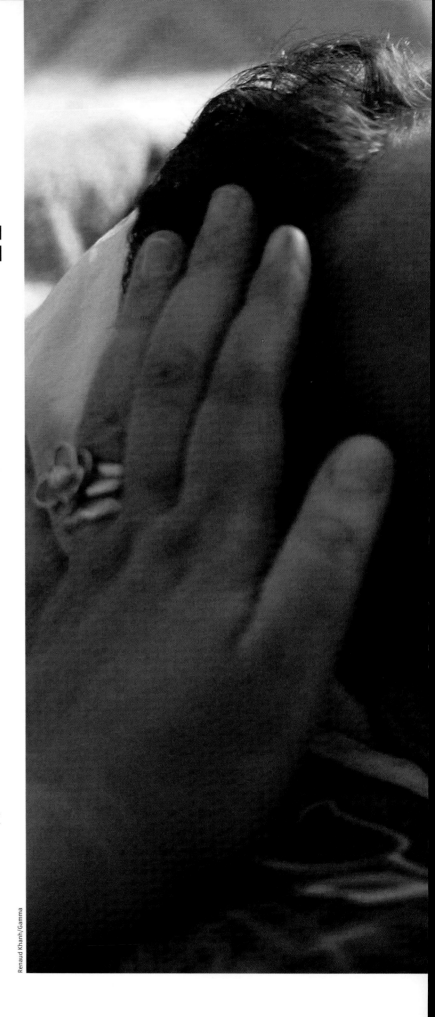

Renaud Khanh/Gamma

### The Daring Rescue of Jessica Lynch

On March 23, Army Pfc. Jessica Lynch, 19, barely survived a firefight in southern Iraq. Having been shot and with broken bones, she was taken by Iraqi soldiers to Saddam Hussein Hospital in Nasiriya, where she was put under the care of Dr. Harith al-Houssona, which proved lifesaving. As bombing drew nearer the city, Dr. al-Houssona moved Lynch to a crowded ward in order to shield her from Iraqi agents who would surely come for her before any rescuers could. When Iraqi agents did indeed show up, Dr. al-Houssona said Lynch had died. Meantime, another Iraqi, the lawyer Mohammed al-Rehaief (left, with his family), risked death by telling U.S. authorities he had seen Lynch at the hospital. American Special Forces now had a location, and close to midnight on April 1 they storm the hospital and spirit Lynch down the stairway (above).

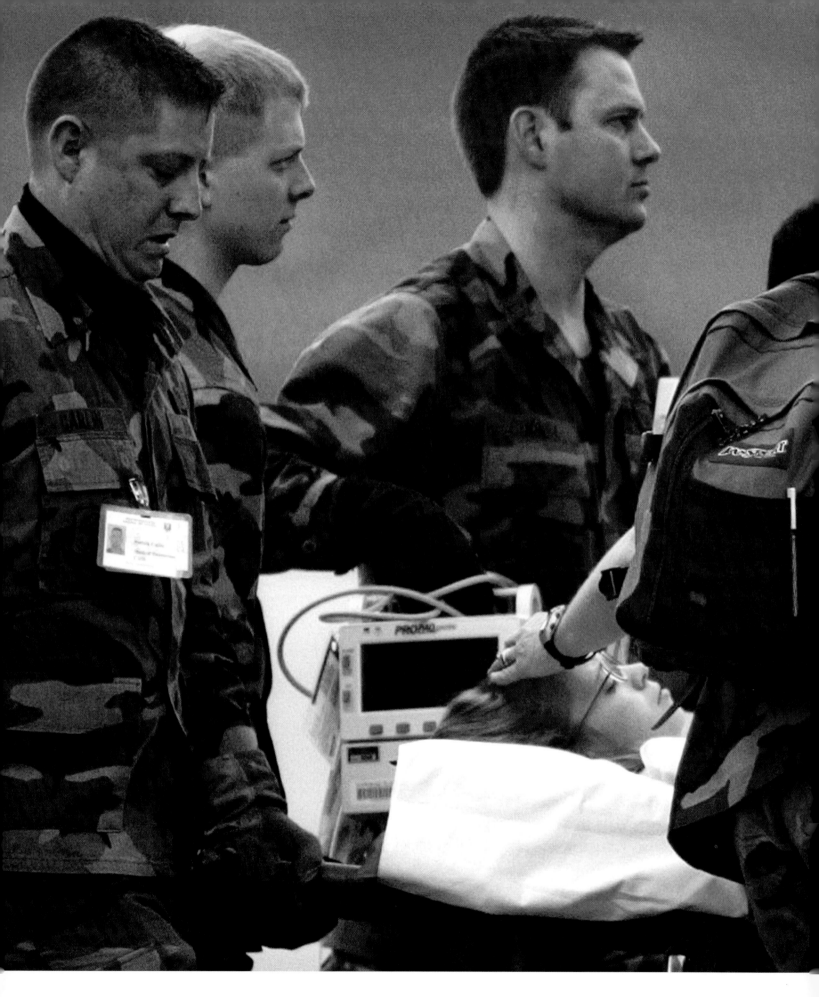

## The Journey Home

After receiving surgery and other treatment at a military hospital in Germany, Lynch is carried to an airplane for transport to the United States. There, military agents (above) have already arrived at the Lynch home in Palestine, W. Va., which has become a site of vigil for neighbors (below), to inform Jessica's parents of her safety. In the aftermath, details distressing and uplifting emerged. During the rescue operation, the Special Forces found shallow graves near the hospital with the remains of 11 people, nine of whom had been with Lynch's unit. On the other hand, the courage of al-Rehaief and Dr. al-Houssona was revealed. While Dr. al-Houssona remained in Nasiriya to tend to other casualties of the war, al-Rehaief was flown with his wife and daughter to the U.S., where he was immediately granted asylum.

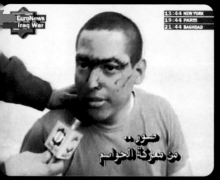

## The Lucky Seven

When that unit from the Army's 507th Maintenance Company took a wrong turn early in the war and became trapped outside Nasiriya, Jessica Lynch wasn't the only one captured. Also taken were (left, from top) Spc. Edgar Hernandez, Pfc. Patrick Miller, Spc. Joseph Hudson, Sgt. James Riley and Spc. Shoshana Johnson, who were paraded before Iraqi TV cameras. Other Americans became POWs during the war, including Chief Warrant Officers Ronald Young Jr. and David Williams, whose helicopter was forced down. On April 12 in Samarra, U.S. Marines, again working on a tip from an Iraqi (this time, a cop), dashed through sniper fire and freed the seven, who were being held together. Above: Williams and Young get support, as does Johnson (opposite). Below: Williams and Young embrace inside a KC-130 transport aircraft.

From left: Sipa (5); Polaris

### Their Spirit Unbroken

Following the same route home as Lynch, the seven are taken to a hospital in Germany, where they wave from a balcony (from left: Young, Miller, Riley, Johnson, Williams, Hernandez and Hudson; Johnson is seated because she has ankle wounds). Left: In El Paso, Tex., Johnson's parents, Eunice and Claude, are relieved that this time the good news is about their daughter. When they had earlier heard about a female POW being rescued, they had initially thought of Shoshana before learning that it was Lynch. Opposite: At Fort Hood, Tex., on April 19, Young, with his dad, shouts to fellow soldiers and points to the shoulder patch of the U.S. Army's 1st Cavalry.

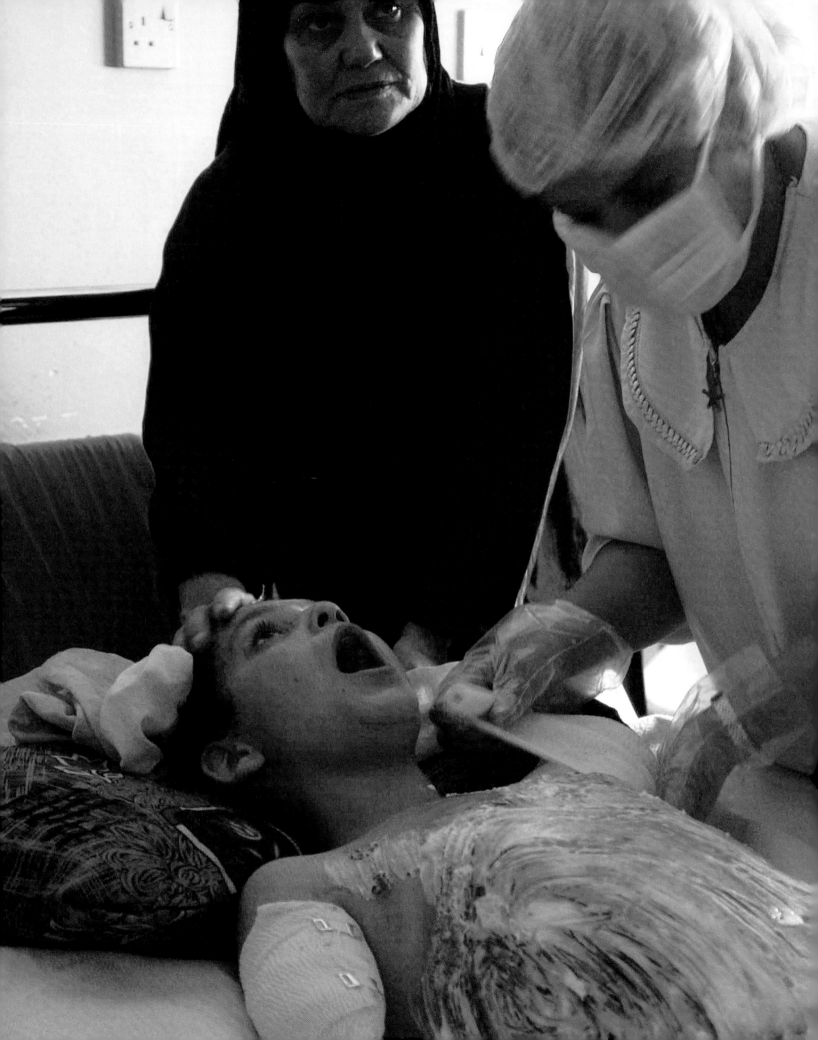

Chris Helgren/Reuters

### The Little Boy Who Became an Emblem of the War

We will never know how many other children suffered fates similar to that of 12-year-old Ali Ismail Abbas, but we know Ali's story, and it must stand in poignantly for all those other innocents killed or injured in the war. Early in the conflict, a U.S. missile landed on the Abbas home, in suburban Baghdad. Ali, who lost most of his family, was left armless, his body horribly burned. His chances of survival were slim at the hospital in Saddam City, where in mid-April a nurse wraps his bandages, and a sheikh plants a kiss. Septicemia, a result of his burns, was spreading bacteria, and Ali required a sterile environment. Finally, evacuation to a burn treatment center in Kuwait City was arranged. As all were painfully aware, that would hardly be the final chapter in Ali's tragically sad story.

Olivier Jobard/Sipa

# Closing In

The Coalition forces were now moving very fast, and in the third week of the war the enemy began to vanish before their eyes.

U.S. Army tanks and Bradley fighting vehicles from the 3rd Infantry roll north near Karbala in central Iraq. Although the Coalition push is in high gear, there are still grave concerns, since no one really knows what awaits in Baghdad.

April 1 **Baghdad** Coalition forces cross into the red zone around the city where they fear they will face chemical and biological weapons.

April 1 **Safwan** Buster, a springer spaniel working for the Royal Army Veterinary Corps, sniffs out a large cache of weapons in a hollowed-out wall. Sixteen Iraqis who had insisted there were no guns are arrested.

April 1 **Baghdad, 9:10 p.m.** Saddam does not appear on Iraqi television for a scheduled speech. Instead, Iraqi Information Minister Muhammad Said al-Sahhaf reads a statement that he claims is from the president: "Hit them! Fight them! They are evil aggressors damned by God. You are victorious and they are defeated."

At left, the Army's 3rd Infantry launches missiles at Republican Guard units located near Karbala, south of Baghdad, on April 2. Opposite: An aerial view of Baghdad, taken at 12:03 p.m. that same day by Space Imaging's IKONOS satellite. The pillars of smoke are billowing from oil-filled trenches that Iraqis have set ablaze. The pollution alone could, over time, kill as many as 5,000 people.

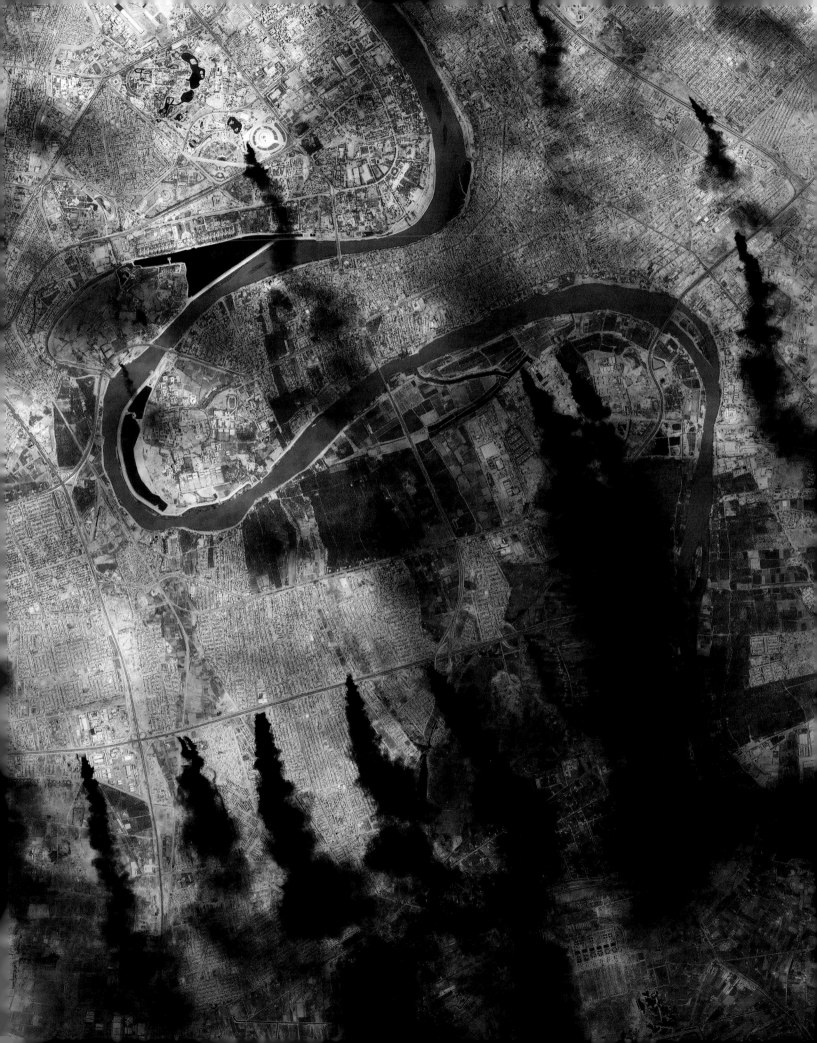

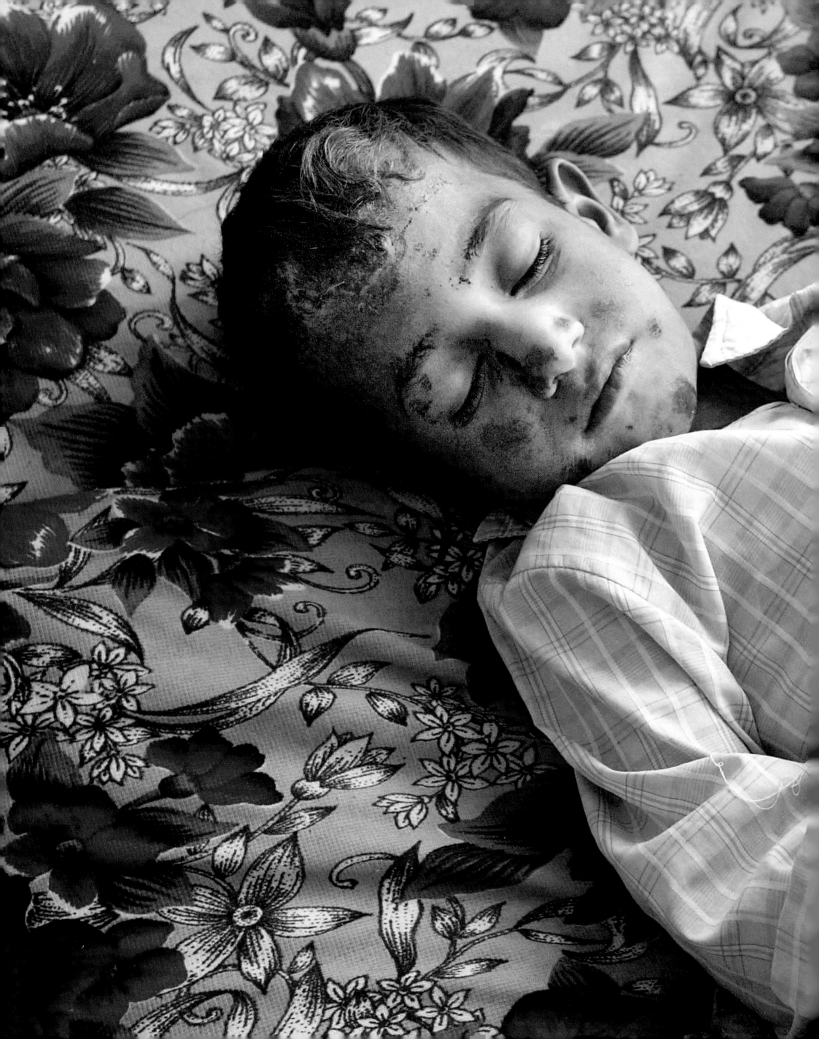

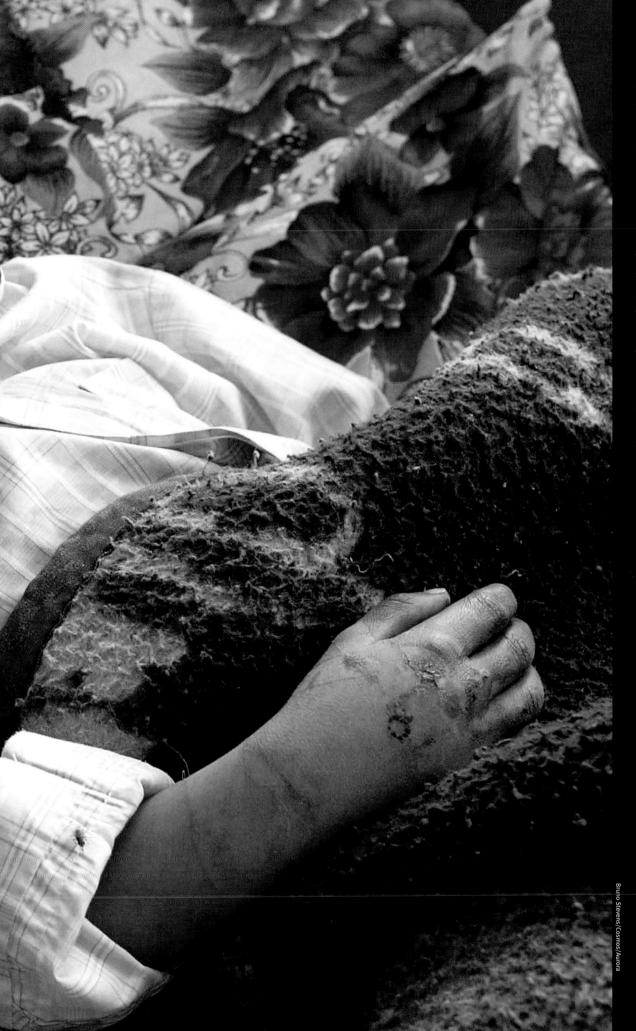

Regardless of the reasons for any war, it is always the suffering of the children that is endlessly regrettable. Here, seven-year-old Hader Ahmed Jassim lies on a mattress in Hilla Hospital in the town of Hilla, not far from Babylon. There are not enough sheets to go around. The boy was hurt when a cluster bomb exploded near his house in the nearby village known as Nader 3. He has a severe concussion and is in total shock.

The British "Desert Rats" are a scrappy lot, but David Toughhill is delighted to help this young Iraqi girl unwrap a piece of candy in the town of Zubayr. At right, also on April 2, British soldiers from Juliet Company, 42 Commando square off in a friendly soccer match near Basra with Iraqi townsmen. According to a retired soldier quoted in *The Washington Post,* it is part of an outreach plan: "First, we have football matches, then we have tea parties, and then somehow our soldiers go out and meet the local ladies." The Brits call American soldiers "Ninja Turtles" because of the Yanks' affection for gear.

April 2 **Nasiriya** Special Forces raid Saddam Hussein Hospital and free Pfc. Jessica Lynch. It is the first successful rescue of an American prisoner of war since World War II. A doctor then leads the forces to shallow graves where they dig up 11 corpses. Nine are from Lynch's unit, including Private Piestewa, the first Native American woman to die in combat

Soldiers from the Army 3rd Infantry Division's "Charlie Rock" Company cover members of Iraq's Republican Guard who surrendered after being outgunned. The one holding his backside was shot during the April 3 skirmish in the outskirts of Karbala.

Christopher Anderson/Vii

The VIP terminal of Saddam International Airport is host to American soldiers from the 3rd Infantry on April 4 as the men move from room to room during a dawn advance on Iraq's capital. Fighting between Iraqi and U.S. forces has been heavy in the battle for control of the important facility, and the machine-gun fire and ear-shattering explosions have produced a chaotic, confusing environment.

April 3 **Baghdad, 9:30 p.m.** U.S. troops attack Saddam International Airport, later renamed Baghdad International. Information Minister Said al-Sahhaf denies the Coalition has taken the airport, suggesting it is a Hollywood "illusion . . . The Americans aren't even 100 miles from Baghdad."

April 3 **Iraq** Retired Army Lt. Gen. Jay Garner, who had overseen the protection of Kurds following the first Gulf War, is tapped to be the administrator of Iraq when this war is concluded. Garner served in Vietnam, and he believes that if the current President had been in charge then, "we would have won."

April 4 **Baghdad** Iraqi TV shows a video of Saddam (or a look-alike) being warmly greeted on the streets of Baghdad.

CLOSING IN **LIFE**

Lieutenant John Blocher and Capt. Andy Maclean of the 3rd Infantry Division's Task Force 2-69 Armor, 3rd Brigade Combat Team out of Fort Benning, Ga., wash off some of the desert dust and grime. They are near Karbala, in a tributary of the Euphrates River. It is April 4, and their unit's morale has received a boost from news of the taking of the airport.

Iraqis exult on April 6 after a U.S. tank is destroyed in Baghdad when 26 M-1 tanks and 10 Bradley armored vehicles suddenly thrust into the heart of the capital city, before stopping at the U.S.-controlled airport. (The crew of the tank was rescued.) Colonel William Grimsley of the 3rd Infantry said the stunning 25-mile sortie, known as Operation Thunder Run, was all about "Let me poke you in the eye because we can, and you can't do anything about it." Greg Kelly of Fox News said that Iraqis played "chicken" with the Americans, driving toward them at 80 mph before being dispatched in the end.

April 4 **Iraq** Said al-Sahhaf says: "We will commit a nonconventional act on them, not necessarily military. We will conduct a kind of martyrdom operation."

April 4 **Iraq** At an American checkpoint, a pregnant woman gets out of her car, screaming. When soldiers approach, the car explodes, killing three Special Operations troops.

April 5 **Baghdad** A convoy of 60 tanks and other vehicles makes a three-hour incursion into Baghdad to demonstrate that the allies can do what they want, when they want.

April 5 **Basra** Coalition forces bomb the home of the notorious chief of Iraq's gas-warfare program, Ali Hassan al-Majid, better known as Chemical Ali. The Brits say they think they've found his body.

As enemy fire crackles around them, members of the 3rd Battalion, 4th Marine Regiment exhort their comrades to charge across the Diyala Bridge. The span, which Americans dubbed the Baghdad Highway Bridge, crosses the Diyala River just southeast of Baghdad. The bridge wasn't strong enough to support tanks, so it had to be taken by foot. Two Marines were lost in the fighting, which took place on April 7.

April 5 **Saudi Arabia** In response to reports that air strikes are "softening up" Iraqi troops, Lt. Gen. Michael Moseley, the top Air Force officer in the war, says, "I find it interesting when folks say we're softening them up. We're not softening them up, we're killing them."

April 6 **Iraq** An American fighter plane mistakenly hits a Kurdish convoy outside Mosul, killing 17 Kurds and one American in the worst friendly-fire incident of the war.

April 6 **Nasiriya** The Pentagon flies in revolutionary Ahmad Chalabi and about 500 members of his Iraqi National Congress to join the fight. Chalabi is seen as a potential candidate for leadership after the war.

April 6 **Basra** British forces launch a nighttime attack on the city and destroy Baath Party headquarters.

April 6 **Baghdad** The first Coalition plane lands at the newly named Baghdad International Airport.

April 7 **Baghdad** Acting on a tip that Saddam and his sons are there, Americans drop four bunker buster bombs on the wealthy sector of Mansur.

For this Iraqi, the Baghdad Highway Bridge on April 7 proved a bridge too far, as the firefight delivered a fatal blow. The Marines fighting for the bridge took no chances, as they had been told by an officer that the enemy had resorted to filling ambulances with explosives. American Marines also came across members of Saddam's elite Republican Guard trying to escape from the city by going over the bridge disguised as civilians.

April 7 **Basra** British troops are greeted warmly as they seize control of the city. Looting begins.

April 7 **Baghdad** Information Minister Said al-Sahhaf says, "The infidels are committing suicide by the hundreds on the gates of Baghdad . . . As our leader Saddam Hussein said, 'God is grilling their stomachs in hell.'"

April 8 **Baghdad** In the advance on Baghdad, American tanks fire on reporters in three locations, including the press center at the Palestine Hotel. Soldiers say they were responding to fire; reporters at the scene say otherwise.

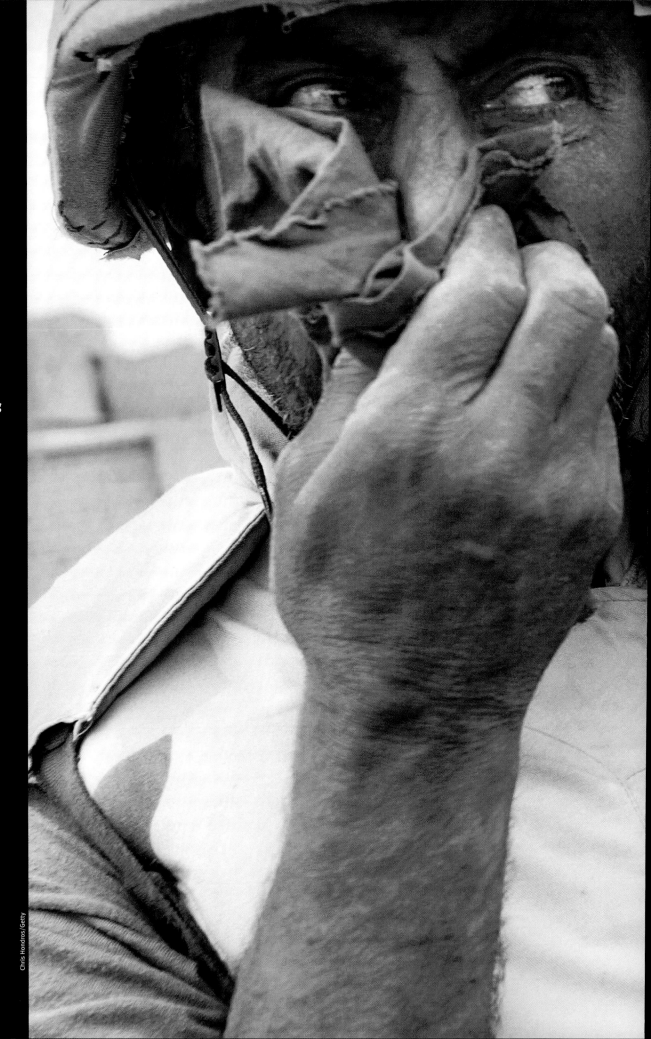

Khudair al-Amiri reunites with his 16-year-old son. He has not seen his boy or the rest of his family since 1991, when he had to flee Iraq after he led an uprising against Saddam Hussein. He ended up in Seattle, where he became a member of the Free Iraqi Forces, a group that provided the U.S. government with translators to help in the war effort. Al-Amiri was traveling with the 24th Marine Expeditionary Unit when it entered Qal'at Sukkar, his hometown, on April 7.

Chris Hondros/Getty

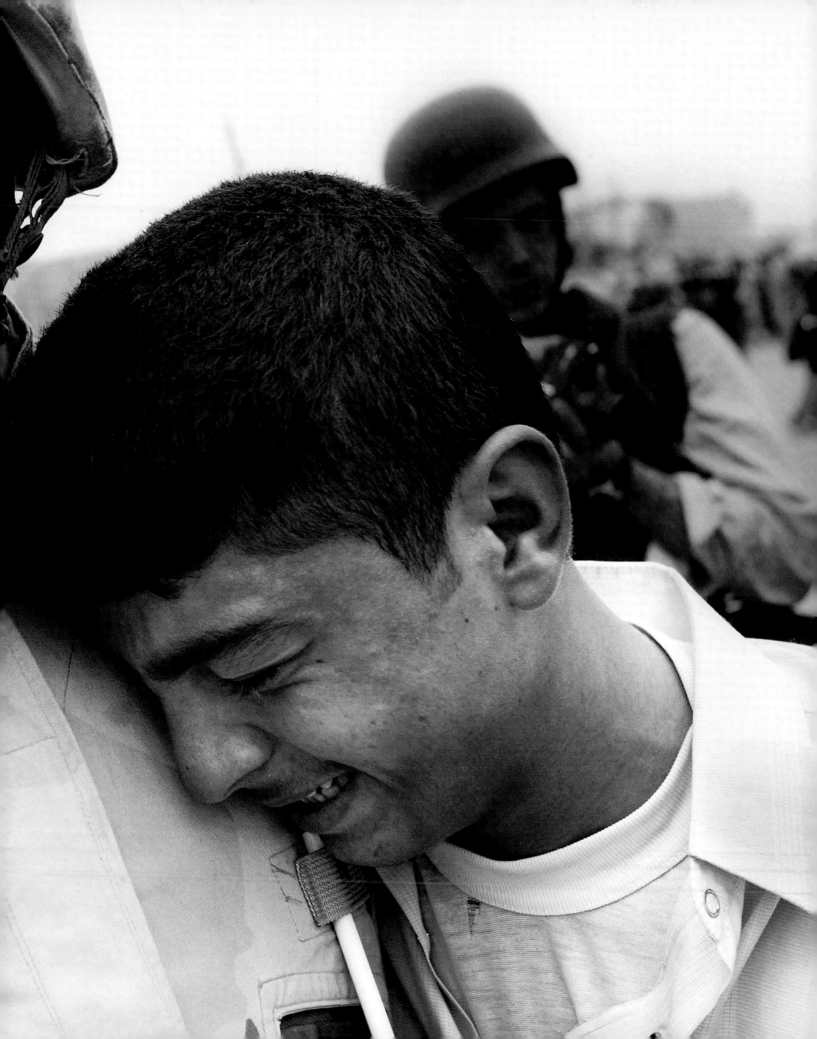

# BRUNO STEVENS'S WAR

**F**our and a half years ago, a Belgian recording engineer had an epiphany: He might better serve society by following his passion for photography, and bear witness to great or tragic world events. At that moment, Bruno Stevens is reinvented as a crusading photojournalist, and he immediately books a flight to Mexico to cover an uprising in the rural districts. From there, his new life takes him to the grim prisons of Haiti, to Serbia, twice to Chechnya, regularly to Israel and the West Bank—and to renown as a documentarian of war and injustice. He wins awards in 2001 for his reports from Chechnya, and again in 2003 for his coverage of Hindu-Muslim rioting in India. In October 2002 he goes to Iraq for a month, and he can feel what is in the air. He returns in February 2003 and hunkers down in Baghdad, waiting for the drama to unfold. As it does, over days and weeks, the imminence of war becomes all too powerfully clear, and then the bombs start falling. By the time they do, Stevens is at home in the city, and is photographing his neighbors. "I have become a Baghdadi myself," he acknowledges. "My purpose is to bring the fate of people in difficult situations to light. Here, it is to show how the people of Baghdad survive this war, from their point of view."

**"In early March there is a parade on Palestine Street. There are perhaps 20,000 soldiers. In the middle are a hundred Fedayeen in white, the color of death and purity. These are the kamikazes, ready and hoping to sacrifice their lives for Saddam and Iraq."**

Cosmos

> **The mood is turning grim. At the arch, 35 miles from the city, teachers from Babylon arrive with the children. The war is coming, so school is closed. In another year, this place would be crowded on this day. The teachers are trying to prove to the children that you can't be afraid.**

The drumbeat grows louder, Baghdadis hear it, life goes on. Above: In February, men take in the races at the Equestrian Club, as always. Right: In March, Iraqis picnic at the arch of Ctesiphon to begin the holy month of Muharram, as always. Below: a new scene. Neya, 10, cries as her aunts and baby cousin flee to Jordan.

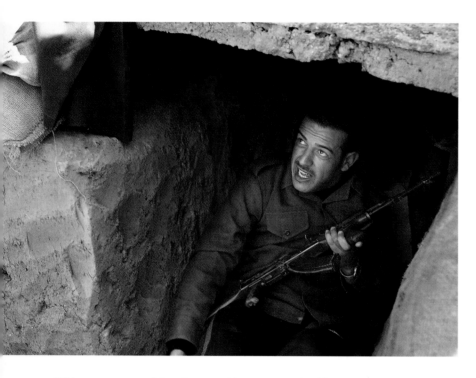

With war on, everything changes. Above: An Iraqi soldier watches the sky during an air raid on March 22. Right: Days later in the Moussa Khadoum mosque, families mourn the 52 victims of a missile that hit a market. Below: At Yarmouk Hospital, Zuhama Abdel Mahmoud sits with her niece Azzra Ismail, six, who has been burned in a cluster-bomb attack. Seven in Azzra's family were killed.

> "I get to the market very shortly after it has happened. It is a bloodbath, and It seems half the dead are children. I follow a family into a neighboring mosque. They are grieving horribly, there is such distress. A mother has lost her daughter, a boy has lost his sister, and they weep. Such a thing, in the poor section. And the children . . . the children pay a high price in war."

"The power is out all over town, and the people can't make bread at home. In the bakeries, they're using generators or even firewood, and suddenly the breadlines grow and they are there all day long, and the lines are constant. The people are afraid. They are poor, and wonder how long they'll be able to afford the bread. The future is an immense question."

A statue of Saddam in an artist's workshop has not been defaced, it is merely unfinished, yet it seems portentous. Above: in a bombed-out courtyard, items of no further use—a Saddam sign and a helmet. Below: Lacking electricity, people can't cook, so a breadline forms on Al-Rashid Street in Baghdad.

BAGHDAD 2003

# Free

A regime is toppled, and
Iraq's next tumultuous
chapter begins.

Goran Tomasevic/Reuters/Landov

On April 9, an American soldier and the citizens of Baghdad are present for the fall of Saddam.

Although looting in a postwar environment is as old as war itself, the repeated images of rabid thievery and the pilfering of ancient artifacts (though not as many as originally thought) made this war's plundering seem somehow more decadent. Further, the rampant lawlessness came to symbolize the concerns held by many that the Coalition launched its attack without having a solid postwar plan.

April 9 **Baghdad** Iraqis attack the statue of Saddam Hussein in Firdos Square. They start off with a sledgehammer and a rope, and eventually U.S. Marines help out. Despite orders not to show the flag, a Marine drapes Saddam's face with the Stars and Stripes—an image that the Arab media focuses on. The flag is replaced with a pre–Gulf War Iraqi flag, then the statue is toppled. Frenzied Iraqis stomp on the statue, then ride the detached head through the streets.

April 10 **Kirkuk** Kurds capture this northern city.

April 10 **Baghdad** Looters break into government buildings, the German embassy and the French cultural center.

April 10 **Najaf** A mob murders a U.S.-backed Shiite cleric in the Ali Mosque.

April 10 **Baghdad** U.S. forces find a cache of weapons that Iraqi forces hid in a school just before the war. It contains dozens of suicide bomber vests.

April 11 **Karbala** In the continuing hunt for banned weapons, U.S. troops unearth 11 shipping containers that hold chemical processing equipment.

Sergeant Roscoe Archer of the U.S. Army's 3rd Division takes a catnap in Saddam's Republican Palace in Baghdad on April 14. Though he may be catching a little shut-eye, the NCO's weapon is, of course, at hand. Saddam's erstwhile palace, which overlooks the Tigris, covers 1.7 square miles. Its size was tripled in the late 1990s. Saddam had eight primary palace compounds.

April 11 **Baghdad** Mobs loot everything they can get their hands on, no longer just targeting Saddam's property.

April 11 **Washington** Donald Rumsfeld downplays looting, comparing it to the gains in freedom: "It's untidy . . . and freedom's untidy, and free people are free to commit mistakes and to commit crimes and to do bad things."

April 12 **Baghdad** The National Museum is looted. Artifacts dating back 7,000 years are taken or destroyed.

April 12 **Baghdad** General Amer al-Saadi, who once ran Iraq's chemical weapons program, surrenders to U.S. forces on hearing he is on their 55-most-wanted list. He says Iraq no longer has chemical or biological weapons.

April 12 **Iraq** U.S. forces stop a bus heading toward Syria with 59 young men carrying $650,000 and a letter offering bounty for killing U.S. soldiers.

April 13 **Tikrit** U.S. forces enter Saddam's claimed hometown, the assumed last bastion.

April 13 **Baghdad** Looting tapers off and Marines start interviewing applicants to police the city and run public utilities.

A U.S. Marine finally finds the time to attend to his laundry on April 14. He is in Tikrit, a former stronghold of Saddam Hussein, and the city he claimed to be his birthplace. Behind the Marine is part of the former summer residence of Saddam, a two-square-mile spread with some 150 sandstone buildings ornamented with verdant palm gardens.

April 14 **Tikrit American forces overrun the city near Saddam's ancestral home. Contrary to expectations, they meet little resistance. Tikrit is the last major target to come under Coalition control.**

April 14 **Baghdad U.S. Marines begin joint patrols with Iraqis.**

April 14 **Washington The war is, for all intents and purposes, finished, says Army Maj. Gen. Stanley A. McChrystal: "The major combat engagements are over because the major Iraqi units on the ground cease to show coherence."**

April 15 **Washington President George W. Bush, following the advisories of his generals, says with confidence: "The regime of Saddam Hussein is no more."**

Twenty-four-year-old Raouf was Saddam's servant for eight years. On April 15 he revisits the Tikriti palace. Above, he checks out one of Saddam's bathrooms. At right, he totes a picture of Saddam and his wife, Sajida Khairallah Tulfah. At left, Raouf surveys the damage inflicted by a Tomahawk missile.

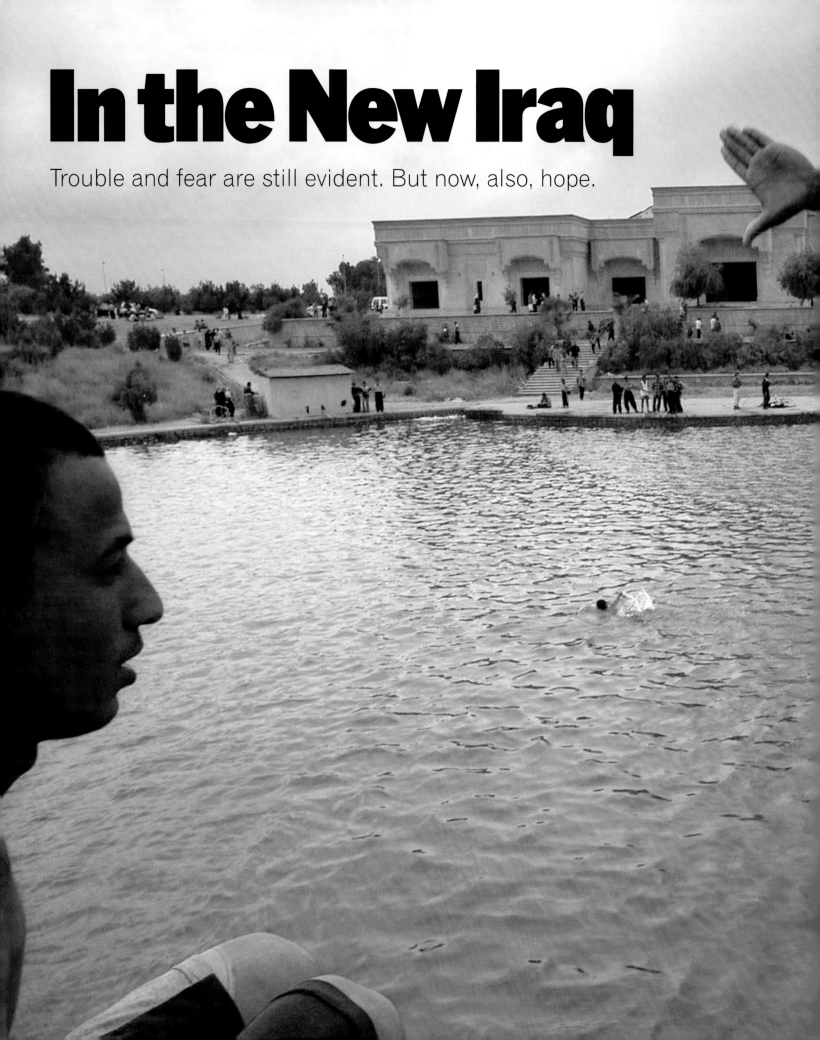

# In the New Iraq

Trouble and fear are still evident. But now, also, hope.

In Mosul, Iraqis dive headfirst into a kingly pool that recently belonged to Saddam Hussein, who allowed no public swimming here.

Lynsey Addario/Corbis Saba

**National Museum Deputy Director Mushin Hasan sits with head in hands as he contemplates all that has been lost to the looters. Coalition soldiers swooped in to help, but too late.**

Immediately after the war, nothing was easy, little was clear. In most sectors there was disorder, in some, chaos. There was tension, there was fear. But there was also the spreading knowledge that Saddam Hussein's reign was truly over, and that what was being promised was freedom.

There was, as the smoke was still lifting, a surrealness to the situation. A self-proclaimed mayor of Baghdad was arrested by American troops because he had been warned against propping himself up as mayor. General Tommy Franks, puffing away on an appropriately large cigar, convened a meeting of his top brass in a Saddam palace where the dictator himself had often held powwows. Kurds and communists distributed newspapers for free on the streets of the capital, and Sunnis and Shiites came together to protest for a common cause. "Muslims, unite against the infidels!" one shouted, meaning the Western conquerors—the Coalition troops that had liberated the streets precisely so such demonstrations might

be staged. In a few instances, pro-Saddam demonstrations by Sunnis turned violent, U.S. Marines opened fire and there were postwar deaths.

The National Museum in Baghdad was looted, and while the artifacts taken were not as many as first reported, they were of enormous value. It looked like a planned job, Iraqi criminals ripping off their country's heritage. Other reports stated that Saddam's family withdrew—stole—as much as a billion dollars from the Central Bank on the eve of war: a last cynical act by a thoroughly corrupt regime that always had power, and never the national interest, as its motivation.

The lights began to come back on in Baghdad, finally, but in many neighborhoods they illuminated scenes of destruction and crime. Soldiers did what they could, but they weren't cops and weren't deployed as such. Municipal employees filtered back to work eventually, and in one of the uplifting signs of a new Iraq, children returned to their schools—schools that would no longer be teaching the lessons of Great Uncle.

**While General Franks (with hands folded) makes plans for reconstructing Iraq in a Saddam palace, U.S. Marines stand guard outside a barbershop in Kut as a boy gets a trim.**

Past, present, future: A woman walks among unearthed graves in al-Karkh Cemetery outside Baghdad, which is filled with Shiites killed by Saddam. Left: Shiite pilgrims in Karbala.

Interesting people were in interesting places: General Franks in Baghdad, U.S. Defense Secretary Donald Rumsfeld in Basra, Secretary of State Colin Powell in Damascus (warning Syria that it better shape up) and President George W. Bush, on May 1, aboard the USS *Abraham Lincoln* off California, proclaiming, "The Battle of Iraq is one victory in a war on terror that began on September 11, 2001, and still goes on." Still going on, too, was a hunt for weapons of mass destruction in Iraq and, in some corners, a continuing search for the complex reason that America went to war.

Whatever the motivation, the outcome was the same—a campaign had been waged and won, a regime toppled and, now, the awesome task of rebuilding was begun. It was surely a good thing that Saddam Hussein would not be part of Iraq's future. And it was surely a good thing that, should dreams of democracy come true, a land of Iraqi self-rule would be a better place than a land under a dictator's thumb. And the cost? Yes, there had been a high cost, but at war's end there was this, which was not insubstantial: the promise, and promises, of liberty.

**On April 27, the al-Amtithal Elementary School is the first to reopen in Baghdad, and friends Fatma Muhammad and Zubaida Salman hug. Most of the 1,200 students stay away out of fear.**

# COMING HOME

On April 19, 2003, U.S. Army Chief Warrant Officer Ronald Young Jr., his POW ordeal over, is back in the embrace of his family at Fort Hood, Tex.

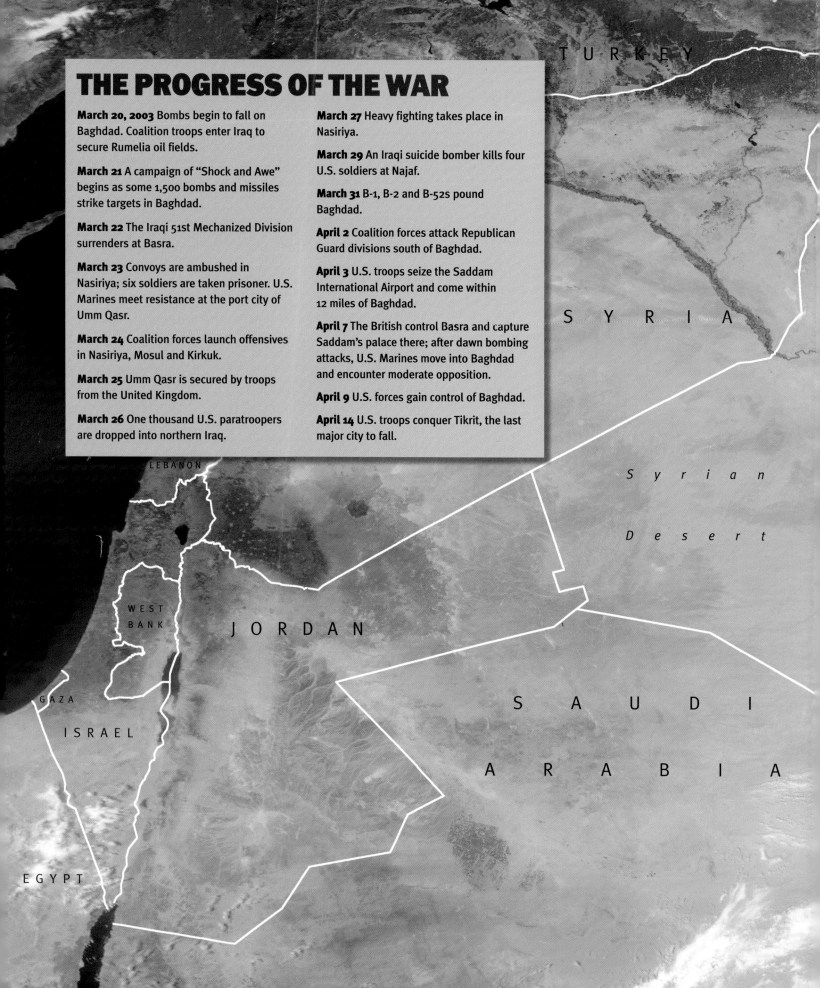

# THE PROGRESS OF THE WAR

**March 20, 2003** Bombs begin to fall on Baghdad. Coalition troops enter Iraq to secure Rumelia oil fields.

**March 21** A campaign of "Shock and Awe" begins as some 1,500 bombs and missiles strike targets in Baghdad.

**March 22** The Iraqi 51st Mechanized Division surrenders at Basra.

**March 23** Convoys are ambushed in Nasiriya; six soldiers are taken prisoner. U.S. Marines meet resistance at the port city of Umm Qasr.

**March 24** Coalition forces launch offensives in Nasiriya, Mosul and Kirkuk.

**March 25** Umm Qasr is secured by troops from the United Kingdom.

**March 26** One thousand U.S. paratroopers are dropped into northern Iraq.

**March 27** Heavy fighting takes place in Nasiriya.

**March 29** An Iraqi suicide bomber kills four U.S. soldiers at Najaf.

**March 31** B-1, B-2 and B-52s pound Baghdad.

**April 2** Coalition forces attack Republican Guard divisions south of Baghdad.

**April 3** U.S. troops seize the Saddam International Airport and come within 12 miles of Baghdad.

**April 7** The British control Basra and capture Saddam's palace there; after dawn bombing attacks, U.S. Marines move into Baghdad and encounter moderate opposition.

**April 9** U.S. forces gain control of Baghdad.

**April 14** U.S. troops conquer Tikrit, the last major city to fall.

# DAYS THAT SHOOK THE WORLD

# TIANANMEN SQUARE

## 4 JUNE 1989

### Jane Bingham

*HODDER*
*Wayland*

an imprint of Hodder Children's Books

# DAYS THAT SHOOK THE WORLD

Assassination in Sarajevo
The Chernobyl Disaster
D-Day
The Dream of Martin Luther King Jr
The Fall of the Berlin Wall
The Freeing of Nelson Mandela
Hiroshima

The Invasion of Kuwait
The Kennedy Assassination
The Moon Landing
Pearl Harbor
The Russian Revolution
Tiananmen Square
The Wall Street Crash

Produced by Monkey Puzzle Media Ltd
Gissing's Farm, Fressingfield
Suffolk IP21 5SH, UK

First published in 2003 by Hodder Wayland
An imprint of Hodder Children's Books
Text copyright © 2003 Hodder Wayland
Volume copyright © 2003 Hodder Wayland

Series Concept:   Liz Gogerly
Commissioning Editor:   Jane Tyler
Editor:   Patience Coster
Picture Researcher:   Lynda Lines
Design:   Jane Hawkins
Consultant:   Michael Rawcliffe
Map Artwork:   Michael Posen

Cover picture: A student in Tiananmen Square challenges the driver of a tank to run him down.

Title page picture: Students in Shanghai taking part in a nationwide protest in December 1986.

We are grateful to the following for permission to reproduce photographs:
Alamy 39 bottom (View Stock); Associated Press 31 bottom; Camera Press 17 top left (W. McQuitty); Corbis *front cover* (Bettmann), 6 (Peter Turnley), 7 (Peter Turnley), 14 (Tod Gipstein), 18 (Peter Turnley), 21 (Peter Turnley), 28 (Jacques Langevin/Sygma), 32 (David Turnley), 35 (Patrick Durand/Sygma), 36 (Bettmann); Popperfoto 11, 13 (Reuters), 23, 31 top (Reuters), 38 (Reuters), 39 top (Reuters), 41 (Reuters), 42, 43 top (Reuters), 46 (Reuters); Reuters 34 (Andrew Wong), 43 bottom (Andrew Wong); Rex Features 2–3 (Sipa), 9 (Mauro Corraro), 10 (Pacific Press), 12 (Sipa), 17 main image (Sipa), 19 (Sipa), 20 (Sipa), 24 both (Sipa), 25 bottom (Sipa), 26 (Sipa), 27 bottom (Sipa), 29 (Sipa), 30 (Sipa), 33 (Sipa), 40 (Sipa); Topham Picturepoint 8 (UPPA), 15, 16, 22 (AP), 25 top (AP), 37 (AP).

Printed in Hong Kong by Wing King Tong

British Library Cataloguing in Publication Data
Bingham, Jane
Tiananmen Square. - (Days that shook the world)
1.China - History - Tiananmen Square incident, 1989 - Juvenile literature
I.Title
951'.058

ISBN 07502 4415 1

Hodder Children's Books
A division of Hodder Headline Limited
338 Euston Road, London NW1 3BH

# CONTENTS

As midnight approached on 3 June 1989, the vast expanse of Tiananmen Square in China's capital, Beijing, was filled with thousands of young people. For the past two months people had been gathering in the Square to protest against the rigid policies of the Chinese government. Some of the protestors were intellectuals and workers, but most were students – all desperate to see changes in their country.

For most of April and May the atmosphere in the Square had been positive. But by the beginning of June the mood had changed as the government began to take serious action. On the morning of 3 June the government had given orders for the army to clear the Square. Throughout the day there were shootings in the streets as Beijing citizens struggled in vain to block the progress of the tanks.

As night fell, army tanks and trucks were positioned around the Square. A helicopter circled above, blaring out instructions for the protestors to leave. Meanwhile most of the students were huddled together around the People's Monument, ignoring all the warnings, just waiting to see what would happen next.

The students seemed calm, almost resigned; some quietly wrote their wills. There was no sense of panic, even though the steady chatter of gunfire could be heard in the streets around the Square and in the darkness beyond.

Around 2 am there was an ominous rumble. Then, very slowly, the first column of transport trucks rolled into the Square, edging forwards at walking pace. Groups of foot soldiers dressed in riot gear and carrying rifles marched beside the trucks.

A sea of protestors in Tiananmen Square in May 1989, when the protest was at its largest.

Gradually, as if in slow motion, hundreds of troops started pouring into the Square. Then they began to spread out in all directions, scattering bullets as they went. A student later reported that in the first five minutes he saw about twenty people hit by stray bullets. He said: 'The soldiers were jumping for joy, as if playing a game.'

Three hours later, the Square was completely emptied of students. Hundreds of young people had been killed or wounded, mostly from gunshot wounds, but some had suffered terrible deaths and injuries, crushed under tanks. Meanwhile, thousands of people of all ages had been killed and injured in the streets around the Square.

Within hours, people around the world were reading news reports of the crackdown and watching TV images of the chaos in the streets. People everywhere reacted with horror and the students became international heroes. Even today, the effects of the Tiananmen crackdown are still being felt.

Chinese soldiers struggle to hold back a wave of students heading for Tiananmen Square.

## Last Words

"On the night of 3 June my son let go of my hand, and ran off to ride his bike to Tiananmen. This was his only hope. His classmates told us that before he died he shouted, 'Don't use force against the people.' When he was shot he said to his classmates, 'I think I may have been shot.' He thought that he had been hit by a rubber bullet. He didn't think it could have been a real bullet that pierced his heart."

*Ding Zilin, mother of Jiang Jielian, a 17-year-old high school student who was killed in Tiananmen Square.*

The Gate of Heavenly Peace leads from Tiananmen Square into the Forbidden City, the home of China's emperors for more than five hundred years.

## The Square of Heavenly Peace

Tiananmen Square was originally built in 1651 as a courtyard for the Forbidden City, the vast palace of the Chinese emperors. It is named after the main gate of the palace, which stands at the northern end of the Square. Tiananmen means 'Gate of Heavenly Peace' in Chinese. In the 1950s the Square was enlarged to four times its original size and covered in cement.

THE TIANANMEN SQUARE PROTEST WAS A reaction to the policies of the Chinese government in the 1980s. But the students' rebellion and the government's harsh response to it also had their origins in China's past. For most of its long history, China had been controlled by very powerful rulers (called emperors) while its people had remained extremely poor and powerless. China was also cut off from the rest of the world for thousands of years. It developed very differently from Western countries, and its rulers were suspicious of Western ways.

Emperors ruled over the kingdom of China for more than two thousand years. They made sure that their people had very little contact with dangerous foreigners. Qin Shi Huangdhi, the first emperor of China, who united his empire in 221 BCE, set a pattern for extremely strict rule that was followed by later emperors. Anyone who disobeyed his orders was brutally punished, and books which contained ideas that contradicted those of the emperor were burnt.

China's emperors lived incredibly luxurious lives in beautiful palaces. Around 1400, a vast walled palace known as the Forbidden City was built in Beijing, but only the emperor's family, advisers and servants were allowed inside it. Meanwhile, most people in China were extremely poor and worked as peasants in the countryside.

By the 1700s, the Chinese emperors had begun to allow trade with Europe. But they were keen to keep foreigners out of China, so merchants were only allowed to trade at the southern port of Canton. The emperors made the merchants pay in silver for Chinese silk, tea and porcelain. But in the 1720s the British started paying with a drug called opium instead. The

emperor was furious and banned all trade with Britain, so the British launched an attack on Chinese ports. Between 1839-42 and 1856-60, China and Britain fought two major wars, known as the Opium Wars, which Britain won. After the British victories, China was forced to allow British merchants to trade at many Chinese ports.

By the beginning of the twentieth century, many people in China resented the power of the emperors and wanted a better life. In 1911, a group called the Kuomintang seized control of China. In the following year, the Kuomintang forced the emperor to abdicate and set up a republic in place of the empire. But not everyone supported the Kuomintang. In 1921 the Communist Party was founded in China. This party, which believes in sharing a country's land and profits equally among all its people, had started first in Russia in 1917. Communism soon became very popular among the ordinary Chinese people, who wanted China to be run by the workers and peasants, rather than by the rich.

Even after his death, China's first emperor still made his power felt. He is buried with thousands of life-sized clay warriors.

ONE GROUP OF COMMUNISTS SET UP THEIR OWN government in the south, and started to share out land between all the people. They were supported by a large band of peasant soldiers led by an energetic young commander – Mao Tse-tung. In 1934, the communists in the south were surrounded by a Kuomintang army. Some of them managed to escape and set off on a long journey to find a safe place for their party to grow. This incredible journey covered 10,000 kilometres (6,000 miles) and is known as the Long March. Later, the story of the heroes who took part in the Long March became an important part of the history of the Chinese Communist Party (CCP).

The struggle between the CCP and the Kuomintang for control of China lasted for more than fifteen years, but eventually the communists took over the government of the country. In 1949, Mao Tse-tung announced the start of the People's Republic of China from the Gate of Heavenly Peace in Tiananmen Square.

Once he was in control, Mao set about reorganizing Chinese society, taking money and power away from the nobles and sharing the country's wealth among its people. In May 1958, Mao started a campaign known as the Great Leap Forward, which aimed to build up Chinese industry very fast. Many peasants were taken away from their farms to work in factories. This meant that not enough crops were planted and millions of people died from hunger.

During the 1960s, Mao became worried that China was becoming too Westernized and that it was moving away from true communism. He was particularly concerned that teachers in schools and universities were spreading Western, capitalist ideas to their students. So he decided to concentrate on the young and, in 1966, started a campaign known as the Cultural Revolution. Mao encouraged young people to be on the look-out for Western-influenced ideas. He urged them to criticize their teachers, parents and bosses if they showed Western sympathies

Mao Tse-tung leads a band of communist supporters. After many years of civil war, Mao emerged as China's first communist leader.

and to report them to Communist Party officials. Many schools and universities were closed, and educated people were forced to work on the land. Groups of teenagers known as the Red Guards took the law into their own hands and beat and tortured anyone they suspected of being against the principles of the Communist Party. After three years of chaos, the army was sent in to stop the violence, but any Western-influenced ideas were still treated with great suspicion.

Altogether, Mao ruled China for twenty-seven years. Despite his numerous mistakes, he was greatly respected by many Chinese people because they believed he genuinely wanted to help his country. However, towards the end of his life Mao became very weak and ill, and his wife Jiang Qing took over the running of the country. Together with three politicians she formed the Gang of Four. The Gang of Four ruled China very strictly, with violent punishments for anyone who disagreed with their ideas, and they were very unpopular.

Chairman Mao waves to the crowds in Tiananmen Square. For twenty-seven years, Mao ruled China with an iron hand.

## Violence and Power

Mao Tse-tung was famous for his sayings, many of which were collected in a little red book entitled *The Thoughts of Chairman Mao*. This book was distributed to everyone in China. One of Mao's most famous 'thoughts' is: 'All power flows from the barrel of a gun.' In this saying, Mao stated his belief that power has to be backed up by violence. Many members of the Chinese Communist Party also believed that it was sometimes necessary to use violence to control the people.

China's President Deng Xiaoping shakes hands with US President Jimmy Carter on his historic visit to the USA in 1979.

AFTER MAO TSE-TUNG'S DEATH IN SEPTEMBER 1976, the Gang of Four remained in power. But within a month they were arrested by the army on the orders of a group of politicians led by Deng Xiaoping (see box opposite). In December 1978, Deng took total control of China, as the country's Paramount (most important) Ruler.

The communist politician Deng Xiaoping was the most forward-looking leader ever to rule China. His main aims were the 'four modernizations' – bringing Chinese industry, agriculture, defence and technology up to date. He tried to move away from the rigid method of controlling the country from the centre; instead he worked to give people more economic freedom to run their own lives. In particular, Deng encouraged farmers to run their farms as businesses, keeping the profits for themselves, instead of simply producing food for the state.

Deng took steps to end China's long isolation from the rest of the world, creating a new 'open door' policy for his country. He started to hold talks with other communist countries, and with the West. In 1978, Deng began negotiations with the United States' government about China's place in the world. In the following year he visited the United States on the first official trip by a senior Chinese leader.

As well as creating links with other countries, Deng made partnerships with foreign businesses, especially companies in Hong Kong, and encouraged them to build offices and hotels in China's towns and cities. Deng's policies had a dramatic effect on life in China. But while some people's lives were greatly improved, the changes also caused problems. By the late 1980s, Deng was facing criticism from many different groups of people in China.

## Deng Xiaoping (1904–97)

Deng Xiaoping joined the Communist Party as a young man and took part in the Long March. In the 1950s he became a member of the Politburo (the decision-making part of the Chinese government). But Deng did not support Mao's policies during the Cultural Revolution and was sent to be 're-educated' into true communist ways by working in a tractor factory. Deng returned to power in the 1970s and by 1974 he was Mao's right-hand man, acting as a leading minister. However, Deng's enthusiasm for more liberal policies – offering the Chinese people more freedom – made him very unpopular with the Gang of Four. In January 1976 he went into hiding for his own safety.

After Mao's death in 1976, Deng made a comeback, overthrowing the Gang of Four and taking control of China. In January 1978, at the age of 73, Deng became China's Paramount Ruler and kept this position until 1987. But even after he retired Deng remained extremely powerful behind the scenes. He was determined to turn China into a modern, forward-looking country, even if the methods he used were not always approved of by other people. He justified his actions in a famous quote: 'It doesn't matter what colour the cat is, so long as it catches the mouse.' After the Tiananmen Square crackdown, many people remembered this saying of Deng's.

President Deng inspects his troops from his official car. Deng used the army to keep firm control of China.

During the 1980s, life became especially hard for people in China's cities.

DENG XIAOPING'S CHANGES IN CHINA CREATED new opportunities for many people. In the country, farms began to prosper after years of neglect, and some farmers became rich. In cities and towns, some enterprising shopkeepers and restaurant owners began to make a profit, and people involved in the newly set up businesses made money fast. But these changes also caused a lot of problems.

As the farmers became more successful, they raised the price of food; this meant that many workers in the towns could no longer afford to buy enough food to support their families. In particular, government workers and teachers were very badly affected because their wages did not rise. All over the country, the gap between rich and poor widened, as some people profited from the changes while others suffered.

There were stories of bribery and corrupt deals between the government and its foreign business partners. Many people were suspicious of China's involvement with foreigners and thought the country was becoming dangerously 'Westernized'.

Under Deng's government, intellectuals (writers, teachers and students) had very little power or status. They were also bitterly disappointed in Deng's reforms. After the Cultural Revolution came to an end they had hoped they could enjoy greater social freedom and be allowed to say what they thought and meet who they liked. But Deng's government kept a firm control on people's lives. The activities of intellectuals were closely watched, teachers in schools and universities were still forced to teach party slogans, and newspapers still carried the government's message. In many cases, government officials continued to choose people's careers, giving them work placements – often against their wishes. This method was used especially to punish people whose ideas were threatening to the government. Students with radical ideas could be sent to work on farms in the country, far away from their friends and family.

While many people in China were growing restless, the rest of the communist world was starting to change dramatically. In 1985, Mikhail Gorbachev became leader of the Soviet Union and introduced two striking new ideas: *glasnost* – more freedom of information, free speech and free elections – and *perestroika* – reform of the way the state was run. These ideas spread rapidly through the communist countries of Eastern Europe. In 1988 thousands of Polish workers went on strike to protest against their government. Poland's communist leaders were forced to allow democratic elections, and the workers' trade union, known as Solidarity, won a huge victory. Poland had ceased to be a communist country.

By the late 1980s, a mood of rebellion was spreading like wildfire through communist Eastern Europe. People openly criticized their communist leaders and turned to Western ideas of democracy as their hope for the future. This new belief that dramatic changes were possible also spread to China. It added to the growing sense that something had to be done to make the government take notice of the people's wishes.

## Calls for Democracy

During the 1980s, many people in communist countries wanted a more democratic society in which individuals had the chance to control their own lives. In particular, they wanted the following:

- freedom of speech;
- freedom of the press;
- freedom of action (especially the right to choose their own jobs);
- freedom to choose their rulers in elections.

Soviet President Mikhail Gorbachev is welcomed to China in May 1989, two weeks before the crackdown in Tiananmen Square.

ALTHOUGH MANY PEOPLE WERE UNHAPPY WITH THEIR government, it was the students who spoke out loudest. This was not surprising in China, a country with a strong tradition of student protest. In particular, the students of Beijing University had famously made their voices heard in 1919 in a protest called the May 4 Movement (see box).

In the late 1970s, Deng Xiaoping began his four modernizations of agriculture, industry, defence and technology. But Chinese students and their teachers were anxious for a fifth modernization – of Chinese society. In autumn 1978, students began to display posters on a stretch of wall close to the centre of Beijing. The posters called on the government to make changes in society and the wall became known as the Democracy Wall. It was used by protestors of all ages to

## A Moment in Time

It is early morning in Beijing on 4 May 1919, and Tiananmen Square is thronging with young people waving tall banners. Thousands of students from Beijing's universities have gathered in the Square to protest against the terms of the Treaty of Versailles (an agreement signed by the Western powers at the end of the First World War). They feel that everyone in China should share their outrage that Chinese land previously held by Germany will be given to Japan rather than returned to China. This kind of public demonstration has never happened before in their country, and people flock to the Square to hear the students' speeches. As they listen, many of them experience for the first time a new sense of patriotism (national pride).

The May 4 Movement of 1919 (shown in this photo) led to widespread debate about China's social and political problems, and the protesting students soon became national heroes.

Workers and students in Beijing study posters on the Democracy Wall.

Students gather in Shanghai as part of a nationwide protest in December 1986.

publish their grievances against the government. Although the posters called for democracy, Chinese students did not want to set up a Western-style government. Almost all of them were loyal communists, who hoped to reform the party by pointing out its problems.

The Democracy Wall in Beijing gave hope to many people throughout the country. By February 1979, underground magazines critical of the government were circulating in several Chinese cities. Young people gathered together in parks, where they read their poetry and sang and danced to the music of guitars. The meetings had a serious, political aim – the students were demanding more freedoms – but they were also relaxed and cheerful events. But this hopeful movement was short-lived. In a tough speech in March 1979, Deng Xiaoping stated that the activities had gone too far and were interfering with China's progress on the four modernizations. Several Democracy Wall activists were arrested, and one student leader, Wei Jingsheng, was sentenced to fifteen years' hard labour.

During the early 1980s there was a series of student protests against the government, but the most extreme demonstrations took place in 1986. The year had begun hopefully, as Deng's government encouraged intellectuals to put forward their ideas for how society could change. But almost as soon as the debate was opened up, the supporters of social reform in the government were defeated by older and more conservative politicians, who warned against dangerous Western ideas.

This harsh response unleashed a flood of protest from the students. During November and December 1986, they took to the streets in cities around China, demonstrating against the government and calling for democracy. On New Year's Day 1987, thousands of protestors gathered in Tiananmen Square, but their protest was swiftly broken up by police. Deng Xiaoping announced that the young people had been led astray by dangerous troublemakers, who were intent on 'the total Westernization of China'.

A homeless man sleeps rough in the streets of Beijing. During the winter of 1989 many people arrived in the cities, looking for work, and were forced to live on the streets and beg for food.

BY THE END OF 1988, AS DENG XIAOPING'S TEN years of reform drew to a close, China was facing a crisis situation. Farmers were not producing enough food to feed all the people, and prices were rising sharply even though many people were becoming poorer. Unemployed workers from the country had begun to move to the towns, but there was not enough work to go round and many turned to illegal ways of making money. There was also plenty of evidence of corruption among government officials. Deng Xiaoping was old and ill (in 1988 he was 84) and there were rumours that he was losing control of the Politburo.

Life was especially hard for the students. Throughout the 1980s their living conditions had been worsening.

They did not have enough food to eat and student residences were very run down. Courses were rigidly structured and there were often not enough books in the libraries. University campuses were protected by guards against so-called 'hooligans' and the students' lives were very strictly controlled. For example, many students had to obey 'curfews' and return to their hostels very early in the evening. Once the students left university, the career prospects for most of them were bleak, and if they became involved in political action, they knew that they would sacrifice any hope of finding a good job.

While many people in China were becoming restless, Deng Xiaoping was quietly making preparations in case of trouble. As early as 1987 he had started training China's army – known as the People's Liberation Army (PLA) – to be ready to deal with mass riots. During the winter of 1988–89 the PLA and the Security Bureau bought large amounts of riot control equipment, including tear-gas and other crowd-controlling chemicals, stanchions (a type of baton) and protective clothing. Also at this time, selected military and security units began training in crowd control. These specially trained units included the highly skilled 8341 military regiment, which was responsible for guarding Zhongnanhai – the headquarters of the Politburo to the west of Tiananmen Square.

As well as making military plans, the Security Bureau purchased sets of miniature television cameras to be placed at crossroads. These tiny cameras, which had been developed by the Japanese, were smaller than a pencil sharpener. They could be automatically controlled from a central station to transmit pictures from all sides of a traffic intersection. After the Tiananmen Square incident, the government claimed that the cameras were intended for monitoring traffic offences, but they also enabled Security Bureau staff to identify people taking part in any demonstrations.

## Li Peng (1928–)

Li Peng's father was one of the first members of the Chinese Communist Party, but he was killed by the Kuomintang when Li Peng was only three. When he was eleven years old, Li Peng was adopted by the Chinese communist leader Zhou Enlai, and grew up very close to people in power. Zhou Enlai sent the young Li Peng to train as a water engineer, and in 1981 he became minister for electric power. When Deng Xiaoping retired in 1987, Li Peng was made premier (prime minister) of China, and he kept this important post until 1998, when he was 70.

Although he was not one of the oldest members of the government, Li Peng joined forces with a group of older politicians, nicknamed 'the elders'. This group tried to slow down the pace of reform in the country and warned against 'spiritual contamination' – the infection of China's youth with dangerous Western ideas. With the support of the elders, Li Peng was the driving force in suppressing the student protests. He was in charge of the country at the time of the Tiananmen Square crackdown, and made sure that he hung on to power after it was over.

PLA troops train for action. By spring 1989, the PLA was ready to deal with any trouble.

O N 15 APRIL 1989, AN EVENT TOOK PLACE that provided a focus for the students' discontent. Hu Yaobang, the popular former party secretary, died suddenly and students throughout China went into mourning.

Hu Yaobang had been an idealistic politician who had played an important part in the social reforms in China, working hard to give people more responsibility for their own lives. In 1986 he had strongly supported the move towards greater intellectual freedom and when the students had rebelled, he had refused to take action against them. This refusal led to his forced resignation in 1987, and Hu had spent his last years in unwilling retirement.

With Hu's death, the students lost a hero who had championed their rights. They began to gather in Tiananmen Square to commemorate Hu's life and to voice their complaints. They called for democracy, for an end to corruption among officials and for a more open dialogue between the people and their leaders.

On 22 April an official memorial service for Hu Yaobang was held in the Great Hall of the People overlooking Tiananmen Square. Three student representatives demanded to meet Premier Li Peng. They carried a petition containing their requests for a fairer and more open society.

In front of a crowd of around 100,000 students, the representatives knelt on the steps of the Great Hall to present their petition, but the politicians completely ignored them. Greatly angered by this snub, students in many cities began to boycott (stay away from) their classes.

On 26 April the government published a message to the Chinese people through an editorial in the official newspaper, the *People's Daily*. The editorial condemned the student demonstrators, accusing a 'small handful of plotters' of deliberately causing chaos. It also suggested that the government should take a firm approach to restore order and hinted that some 'bloodletting' would 'not be a bad thing'.

In Tiananmen Square a giant portrait of Hu Yaobang is surrounded with flowers and tributes. Hu's death led to a great outburst of emotion in China.

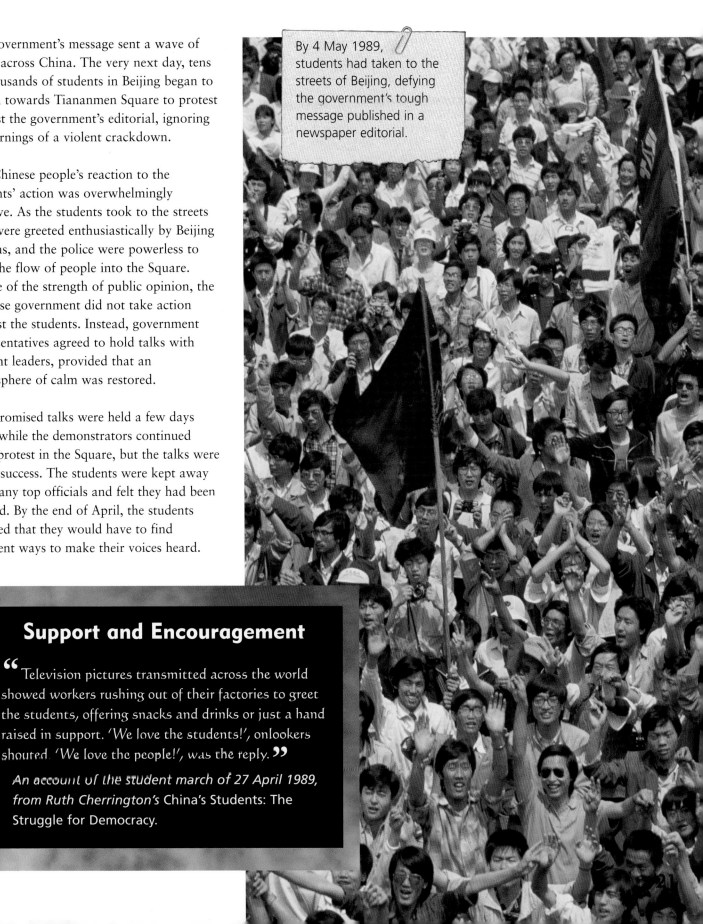

The government's message sent a wave of anger across China. The very next day, tens of thousands of students in Beijing began to march towards Tiananmen Square to protest against the government's editorial, ignoring its warnings of a violent crackdown.

The Chinese people's reaction to the students' action was overwhelmingly positive. As the students took to the streets they were greeted enthusiastically by Beijing citizens, and the police were powerless to stop the flow of people into the Square. Aware of the strength of public opinion, the Chinese government did not take action against the students. Instead, government representatives agreed to hold talks with student leaders, provided that an atmosphere of calm was restored.

The promised talks were held a few days later, while the demonstrators continued their protest in the Square, but the talks were not a success. The students were kept away from any top officials and felt they had been tricked. By the end of April, the students realized that they would have to find different ways to make their voices heard.

By 4 May 1989, students had taken to the streets of Beijing, defying the government's tough message published in a newspaper editorial.

## Support and Encouragement

"Television pictures transmitted across the world showed workers rushing out of their factories to greet the students, offering snacks and drinks or just a hand raised in support. 'We love the students!', onlookers shouted. 'We love the people!', was the reply."

*An account of the student march of 27 April 1989, from Ruth Cherrington's* China's Students: The Struggle for Democracy.

21

On 4 May 1989, dancing students celebrate the seventieth anniversary of the student protests of May 1919.

THE MONTH OF MAY 1989 CONTAINED TWO very important dates. The first was 4 May, the seventieth anniversary of the famous student protest in Tiananmen Square at the end of the First World War (see page 16). The second was 17 May, when President Mikhail Gorbachev of Russia was scheduled to visit China for talks with the Chinese government for the first time in more than thirty years.

On 4 May 1989 around 60,000 students held a lively demonstration in Tiananmen Square with speeches, singing and dancing. The students were joined by workers and journalists demanding fairer working conditions and freedom of the press, and crowds lined the streets around the Square, cheering them on.

On the same day, Party Secretary Zhao Ziyang gave some surprising signs of support for the student movement. In a speech to international members of the Asian Development Bank, Zhao did not condemn the student protests and even acknowledged that some of their demands were 'reasonable'. Zhao was well known for his liberal views. His speech was welcomed by the students as a hopeful sign.

The week following 4 May was relatively quiet, but as the visit of President Gorbachev approached the students decided to take a more dramatic stand. On 13 May thousands of students marched to Tiananmen Square, and several hundred of them announced they were going on hunger strike. They stated that they would refuse all food and stay in the Square until the government agreed to a genuine dialogue with them.

News of the hunger strike brought to the Square crowds of sympathizers who were deeply touched by the young people's sacrifice. The emotional scenes were recorded by cameramen and journalists from all over the world, who were already in China to report on Gorbachev's visit.

Party Secretary Zhao Ziyang visits a hunger striker in hospital. Zhao Ziyang was the only member of the Chinese government to show sympathy for the students.

By the time Gorbachev arrived in China, the government was in a very difficult position. More than 3,000 students had joined the hunger strike, and the government faced the prospect of being held responsible for a large number of young deaths. A planned ceremony in Tiananmen Square was cancelled and the Russian visitors were kept away from the Square as much as possible. But it was impossible to ignore the crowds that had gathered there, and the wail of ambulance sirens as collapsing hunger strikers were rushed to hospital.

On 18 May, Premier Li Peng and Zhao Ziyang visited some of the hunger strikers in hospital and agreed to hold talks with them. Later that day the students arrived at the Great Hall of the People looking exhausted – one was still wearing his pyjamas and carrying a hospital drip! However, no progress was made. Li Peng remained proud and aloof, and in the end the students walked out in disgust.

## The Patriotic Democratic Movement

The Chinese student protest movement of the late 1980s is often known as the Patriotic Democratic Movement. This name reflects the two different aspects of the students' cause. The students campaigned for a more open, democratic society with greater freedom for the Chinese people (see page 15). But they were also patriotic – intensely proud of their country and its history. Almost all the students still thought of themselves as communists and did not want China to become a Westernized, capitalist country.

ON 18 MAY, PRESIDENT GORBACHEV LEFT China. Although the Chinese and Russian leaders had begun to discuss restoring good relations between their countries, it was clear that their talks had been seriously affected by the student action. So, the following morning, Premier Li Peng was in a grim mood when he and Party Secretary Zhao Ziyang visited Tiananmen Square at dawn. Li Peng seemed unmoved by the sight of so many weakened young people and told the students briskly that they should go home. But the more liberal Zhao Ziyang was clearly upset. In a heartfelt and emotional speech he apologized to the students, saying: 'I have come too late'.

Later on in the day, more than a million people took to the streets of Beijing to demonstrate against the government, chanting 'Save the children! Save the nation!'. The city was plunged into chaos and most people stayed away from work. Meanwhile, in the Square the students held a vote on whether to continue the hunger strike. Many of the hunger strikers were now dangerously ill and the students were afraid of what the government might do next. They voted by a narrow margin to call off the hunger strike but to continue occupying the Square.

In the early hours of Saturday 20 May, at a special meeting of the Communist Party congress, a grim-faced Li Peng declared martial law – control by the army – in parts of Beijing. He spoke of the 'turmoil' and 'chaos' caused by the students and of the threat they posed to the security of the country. Li Peng was backed by the elders, including some party officials who were so old they had to be brought in wheelchairs. But the moderate Party Secretary Zhao Ziyang was nowhere to be seen. Clearly, the hardliners had taken control of the government.

A solitary protestor with a rose faces a row of guards in Tiananmen Square.

'I have no voice.' A student wears a gag to show he has been silenced by the Chinese government.

Li Peng set a deadline of 5 am the following morning for the Square to be cleared, after which the army would move in. But the students refused to be frightened away. Some groups drifted off but thousands stayed, apparently ready to sacrifice their lives for their principles. To keep their spirits up, they repeatedly sang the 'Internationale' (the song of the communist movement) and the Chinese national anthem.

Meanwhile, PLA troops waiting on the outskirts of Beijing began to move slowly towards the centre of the city. But before they could make much progress, a squad of young motorbikers known as the Flying Tigers warned the people of Beijing that the army was coming. All over the city, groups of residents rushed out to set up roadblocks, using buses, trucks and dustbins to bar the soldiers' path.

Once the soldiers were no longer able to move, the people started to reason with them, begging them not to hurt the students. Most of the PLA soldiers had no idea what was happening in the city and were easily won over. Only a few scuffles were reported as the army was peacefully stopped in its tracks. Li Peng's attempt to enforce martial law had been foiled by a remarkable show of 'people power'.

A Beijing policeman offers a gesture of support to students on their way to the Square.

## Protecting the Students

**"**We all had the same mind, the same idea. No one told us what to do. We just went out on the streets to stop the army. The Party no longer controlled us.... We all went out to protect the students **"**

*An elderly woman involved in holding back the army in Beijing in May 1989.*

A bus is dragged across a street to prevent troops from advancing further into the city.

Beijing citizens watch helplessly as truckloads of PLA troops roll into the city.

PREMIER LI PENG'S ANNOUNCEMENT OF MARTIAL law on 20 May set off a wave of demonstrations in cities all over China. Meanwhile, on the streets of Beijing there was a new mood of defiance following the successful holding back of the troops. People expressed their support for the students by singing and dancing and chanting slogans. By 23 May all the troops had retreated to the outskirts of Beijing.

However, in spite of the widespread demonstrations a sense of stalemate soon began to set in. The government was clearly not responding to demands, and it had withdrawn once more into unreachable silence. The next meeting of the government congress was not scheduled until 20 June.

By the last week in May, the strain on the student protestors was beginning to show. Many had begun to leave the Square and there were problems finding enough food for those that remained. The students

made determined efforts to organize themselves, forming a committee to coordinate their efforts and establishing a 'Defend Tiananmen Square' headquarters. On 27 May the committee recommended that the occupation of the Square should end by 30 May. However, at the last minute, a group of radical students took over and made a new resolution. They would stay in the Square until 20 June, the date for the next meeting of the government congress.

Despite their determination to continue, the students were desperately in need of a new source of inspiration, and they found it in the shape of a Styrofoam statue. During the night of 29 May the 10-metre-high statue was wheeled into Tiananmen Square, supported on six bicycles. The statue was the work of students at the Central Academy of Fine Arts. It closely resembled the famous Statue of Liberty in New York, and was intended to represent the spirit of freedom and democracy.

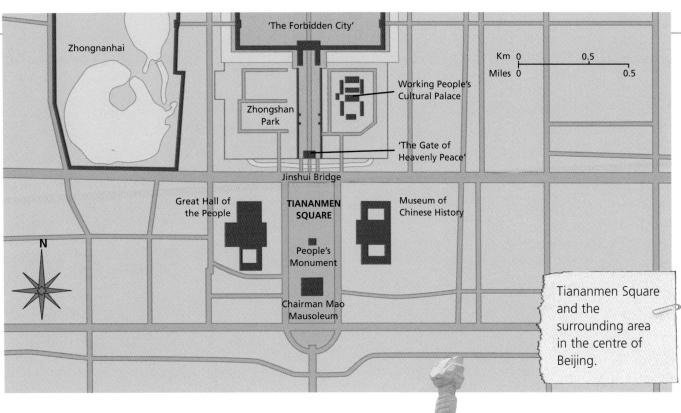

Zhongnanhai

'The Forbidden City'

Working People's
Cultural Palace

Zhongshan
Park

'The Gate of
Heavenly Peace'

Jinshui Bridge

Great Hall of
the People

TIANANMEN
SQUARE

Museum of
Chinese History

People's
Monument

N

Chairman Mao
Mausoleum

Km 0        0.5
Miles 0        0.5

Tiananmen Square and the surrounding area in the centre of Beijing.

In a deliberate act of defiance, the glaringly bright, white statue was placed opposite the huge portrait of Chairman Mao. It was unveiled in a solemn ceremony in front of members of the international press. The statue immediately became a gathering point for the students and a symbol of their struggle and ideals. As one student put it: 'Soldiers will try to knock it down, but not yet. We must protect the statue!'

The vast Styrofoam statue of the Goddess of Liberty, surrounded by students and members of the press.

## Non-Violent Struggle

At the beginning of June, the student protestors were visited by Dr Gene Sharp, an American academic from Harvard University. Dr Sharp, who specializes in the study of non-violent struggle, observed that the students used entirely peaceful methods of protest and resistance. He concluded that they had worked out their non-violent strategy themselves, rather than learning about it from books. But they did have some knowledge of the non-violent methods used by Mahatma Gandhi in India and the Solidarity movement in Poland.

BY EARLY JUNE, MANY OF THE STUDENTS WERE close to collapse. The Square was constantly filled with noise and activity so it was very hard to sleep. Most of the protestors were also suffering from lack of proper food. They had survived for weeks on whatever the citizens could spare – mainly noodles and water – and were now very weak. Everyone in the Square was in a constant state of alert, waiting for the sound of approaching troops.

At 5 pm on Friday 2 June a new hunger strike was announced – it was to be on a much smaller scale than before, but would involve three well-known figures. One of the hunger strikers, Hou Dejian, was a rock star who had been inspired by the students' cause. The presence of Hou Dejian, who came from Taiwan – a country that had broken away from communist China in 1949 – acted as a magnet for the city's young people. All through the evening of 2 June students kept pouring into the Square on their bicycles.

Meanwhile, in other parts of the city PLA troops were clearly visible, preparing to move as soon as they were given the order. There were rumours that soldiers were trying to get on friendly terms with Beijing citizens, but the people remained determined in their support of the students.

On the night of 2 June, two companies of soldiers starting marching towards Tiananmen Square, but neither of them reached the centre. One group was surrounded by citizens and prevented from moving forwards. The other group, accompanied by buses and tanks, was involved in a traffic accident in which two citizens were killed. Surrounded by angry crowds, the soldiers eventually turned back.

Students settle down for the night in Tiananmen Square. Some protestors had tents, but many slept in the open, on the ground.

Soldiers march through the streets of Beijing on 3 June, 1989.

By the morning of 3 June, soldiers were taking up positions close to the Square, although some were still held back by barricades erected by angry citizens in the streets. During the afternoon a series of violent clashes took place between the soldiers and Beijing citizens, the people shouting and throwing stones, while the soldiers shot to kill.

By the evening of 3 June, PLA troops had broken through all the barricades and surrounded the Square. The city was filled with burning vehicles. Hundreds of citizens had been killed in the struggle to hold back the troops – some crushed by tanks and armoured personnel carriers, others shot at point-blank range.

## Student Promise

"I swear to use my young life to protect the Square. Our heads may be cut off, our blood may flow, but the People's Square must not be lost."

*An oath sworn by students in Tiananmen Square on 3 June 1989.*

The Chinese government broadcast a message saying: 'Counter-revolutionary rebellion is now taking place. Ruffians are violently attacking PLA soldiers.... They aim to overthrow the People's Republic of China.' Clearly the government was prepared to take any measures needed to crush the protest. The outlook for the students in the Square looked grim indeed.

Tanks roll into Tiananmen Square in the early hours of 4 June.

BY MIDNIGHT ON 3 JUNE MOST OF THE STUDENTS had withdrawn to the People's Monument in the southeast of the Square where they sat, huddled together, wondering what the next day would bring. They did not have long to wait.

**1.00 am**   People who had witnessed the killing of civilians on the streets of Beijing reported to the students' command headquarters, urging them to leave the Square. But student commander-in-chief, Chai Ling, appealed to the protestors to stay.

**2.00 am**   The first column of troop transport trucks rolled into the Square, moving slowly forwards at walking pace. Accompanying the trucks were groups of foot soldiers wearing steel helmets and carrying assault rifles. The soldiers fanned out slowly along the northern edge of the Square and sealed off the northeast entrance. Some students were shot as the soldiers pressed forward.

**3.00 am**   Thousands of silent soldiers, each armed with a rifle and a long wooden cudgel, positioned themselves around the Square. Only a small exit corridor in the southeast was left open.

With the protestors torn between staying and leaving, two of the hunger strikers – the rock star, Hou Dejian, and the economist, Zhou Duo – began to negotiate with army officials to give the students time to leave the Square safely. The officials stressed that withdrawal had to be unconditional (in other words, the protestors could not make any demands) and the Square had to be emptied by daybreak.

**4.00 am**   Suddenly, all the lights went off in the Square and the statue of the Goddess of Liberty was toppled by a tank. For fifteen minutes there was nothing but darkness and silence. The students remained on the Monument, and no one made a move to leave.

**4.15 am**   The Square was flooded with light again, and the southernmost doors of the Great Hall swung open, releasing a stream of armed troops. These soldiers formed an L-shaped line in front of the Mao Mausoleum and fired warning shots at the Monument.

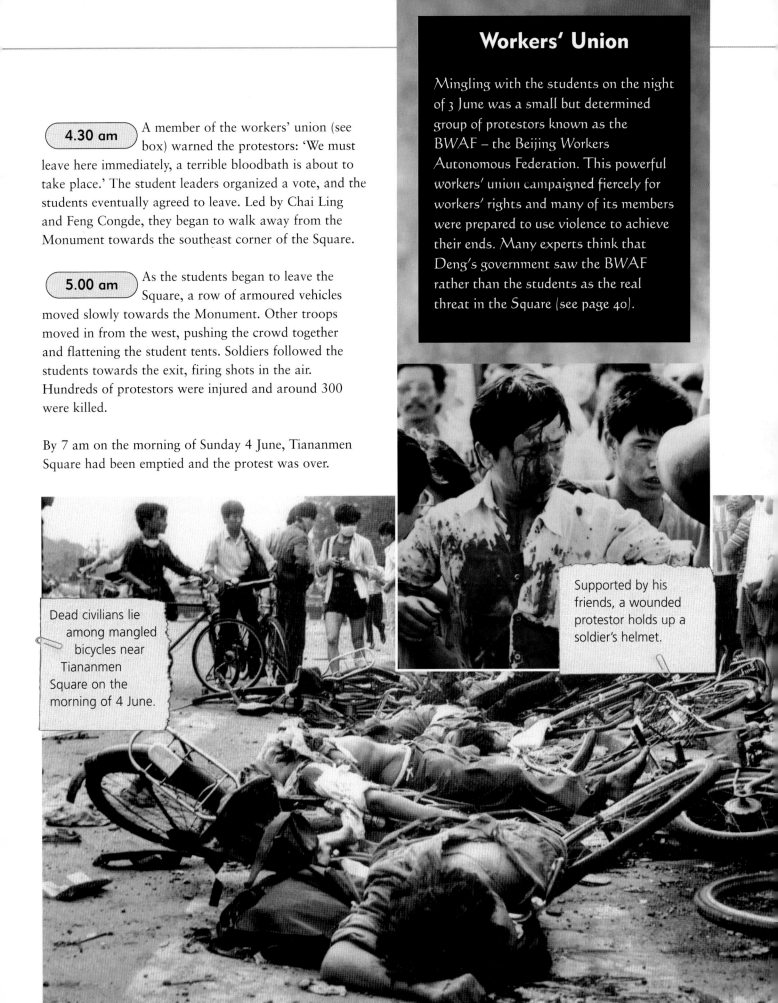

**4.30 am** A member of the workers' union (see box) warned the protestors: 'We must leave here immediately, a terrible bloodbath is about to take place.' The student leaders organized a vote, and the students eventually agreed to leave. Led by Chai Ling and Feng Congde, they began to walk away from the Monument towards the southeast corner of the Square.

**5.00 am** As the students began to leave the Square, a row of armoured vehicles moved slowly towards the Monument. Other troops moved in from the west, pushing the crowd together and flattening the student tents. Soldiers followed the students towards the exit, firing shots in the air. Hundreds of protestors were injured and around 300 were killed.

By 7 am on the morning of Sunday 4 June, Tiananmen Square had been emptied and the protest was over.

## Workers' Union

Mingling with the students on the night of 3 June was a small but determined group of protestors known as the BWAF – the Beijing Workers Autonomous Federation. This powerful workers' union campaigned fiercely for workers' rights and many of its members were prepared to use violence to achieve their ends. Many experts think that Deng's government saw the BWAF rather than the students as the real threat in the Square (see page 40).

Supported by his friends, a wounded protestor holds up a soldier's helmet.

Dead civilians lie among mangled bicycles near Tiananmen Square on the morning of 4 June.

SUNDAY 4 JUNE DAWNED ON A CITY IN CHAOS. The streets were full of mangled metal and broken glass – the remains of the barricades put up to stop the army's progress. A number of roads remained blocked and upturned buses and trucks – many of them still burning – littered the city. Dead bodies lay on the streets around Tiananmen Square, and wounded students were being rushed to hospital in any vehicles that could be found – carts, rickshaws and buses.

The people of Beijing wandered through their city in a daze, unable to believe what had happened. Students searched desperately for their lost companions, while some angry citizens attacked the police and soldiers. Occasional bursts of gunfire could still be heard as soldiers fired at unruly citizens. Meanwhile, Tiananmen Square was a sea of green army uniforms, as the soldiers removed all traces of the student occupation, burning their tents and possessions on large bonfires.

For five days following the crackdown nothing was heard of Deng Xiaoping and rumours began to circulate that he was ill or even dead. Eventually, on 9 June, Deng appeared on television looking very old and shaky. In his speech to the people Deng announced that the government had suppressed a

## Aftermath

**"** I looked over at Tiananmen and wondered how it could have been cleared so quickly…. Thick black smoke rose from the spot where the 'Goddess' had stood…. Beyond the Square in all directions were clouds of smoke and the sound of shooting. It seemed as if the whole city was being destroyed. **"**

*A Western observer describes the scene in Beijing in the early morning of 4 June 1989.*

Wrecked and burnt-out vehicles litter the streets around Tiananmen Square.

'counter-revolutionary rebellion' in which the 'dregs of society' had tried to 'establish a bourgeois republic dependent entirely on the West.'

The government worked hard to spread its version of events through television broadcasts and newspapers. Officials stated that the Square had been cleared peacefully with no loss of life and that the only killings had been of 'thugs' who had attempted to stop the army from carrying out its duty. There were pictures of soldiers cleaning up the city and the troops were praised for their bravery and efficiency. The government also published pictures of leading protestors who had been arrested, looking defeated and humiliated.

After about a week, life in Beijing began to return to normal although everyone had been changed by the crackdown. Citizens were frightened into silence as the government started to arrest activists, sympathizers and 'rumour-mongers'. As a result, people simply stopped talking about the part they had played in the events in and around Tiananmen Square. Gradually all the workers who had gone out on strike in support of the students drifted back to their jobs, afraid of punishment if they stayed away. The students were in mourning for their lost companions, and the atmosphere in the universities was demoralized and cautious. Everyone knew that they were being observed by government agents who were on the lookout for any signs of rebellion.

In this hastily captured photo, student leaders are arrested and led away by police officers.

33

Police watch a peaceful pro-democracy protest in southern China in May 1989. This was part of a massive wave of protests, which took place all over China that year.

ALTHOUGH THE CITY OF BEIJING WAS THE CENTRE of the protests in 1989, the pro-democracy movement spread far beyond the capital. During the 1980s, people all over China had become critical of the government and, by spring 1989, there were demonstrations in cities and towns throughout the country.

The student demonstrations of the 1980s followed the same pattern all over China. Before 1989, there had been occasional protests, mainly about poor living conditions, but these were generally not very large or well organized. However, the death of Party Secretary Hu Yaobang on 15 April (see page 20) provided a focus for the students' discontent. Throughout the country, students held demonstrations to celebrate the life of 'a warrior for the people's cause' and to call on the government to make China more democratic.

The next important trigger for protests across the country was Li Peng's declaration of martial law on 20 May. This resulted in mass demonstrations involving workers as well as students. Some students set up barricades in the streets, and broadcast anti-government speeches.

Finally, the Tiananmen Square crackdown of 4 June 1989 unleashed the biggest protests of all. Massive marches were organized throughout China, as people surged through city centres, some marching and waving banners and others driving trucks plastered with posters.

Although most of the protests in the provinces were non-violent, there were some clashes between protestors and local police. The most famous of these took place in the city of Xi'an, and became known as the 22 April incident. Here, marching students were joined by groups of unemployed young men and the demonstration soon got out of hand. The gatehouse to the government headquarters was set on fire and the fire brigade was called. When the fire brigade turned their hoses on the protestors, a riot developed, and police started charging the crowd, beating the demonstrators with sticks and clubs. Old people, women and children were injured and some shops were wrecked. Witnesses saw police dragging some protestors behind police lines and beating them severely.

The 22 April incident was probably one of the reasons for the harsh government message in the *People's Daily* of 26 April, in which 'hooligans' were blamed for creating 'turmoil and chaos' in China (see page 20).

Despite all the anger unleashed throughout the country in June 1989, the mood of defiance could not last. After the initial reaction to the crackdown had subsided, people across China became demoralized and ceased to protest in public. As in Beijing, students and workers were afraid of the prospect of arrest and discouraged by the lack of any government response. The country settled down again to an uneasy peace.

## A Moment in Time

On the morning of 19 May 1989, a demonstration is turning violent in the streets of Shaoyang City. Someone has set a car on fire and it is burning fiercely. Among the crowd watching the demonstration is a fifteen-year-old school student, Liu Xin, who has been taken along by his brother-in-law to see what is happening in his city. Suddenly, Liu Xin is seized by the police and arrested. He is charged with supplying matches to the demonstrators. Liu Xin protests that he is innocent and says he does not have anything to do with the demonstrators, but it is no use. He is taken off to prison.

(Liu Xin is scheduled to be released in June 2004, aged thirty, after having spent half his life in prison.)

Army tanks move in to break up a demonstration on 8 June. After the Tiananmen crackdown, the Chinese government began to use harsher methods to put a stop to protests.

News of the crackdown in Tiananmen Square soon reached the rest of the world. Television and newspaper reports were full of images of tanks bearing down on defenceless young people. The news agencies announced that thousands of students had been killed on the night of 4 June. In reality, the crackdown left hundreds rather than thousands dead in the Square, but the shocking fact remained that armed soldiers and tanks had been used to break up a non-violent student demonstration. People everywhere were horrified.

In the days following the Tiananmen crackdown, government leaders all over the world spoke out against the Chinese government's actions. US President George Bush imposed an immediate ban on all military sales to China. He also put a stop to any planned visits by Chinese or American military leaders to each others' countries.

## All Change

" During the years 1978 to 1989 China managed to create an image (however inaccurate) as the more human face of communism... [But] the Tiananmen 'crackdown' of June 1989 obliterated newly formed images of China. Particularly in the West there was horror, outrage, revulsion.... The lenses through which China had previously been perceived needed to be refocused. "

*From* China in the 1990s *by Robert Benewick and Paul Wingrove.*

Images like this, of a lone Chinese student facing a row of tanks, were seen on televisions all over the world and caused widespread horror.

US President George Bush took a tough line against China. He is shown here announcing a ban on US military sales to China.

Within a few months, most of the links with foreign countries that Deng Xiaoping had worked so hard to create had been broken. The five years leading to 1989 had seen great progress in Chinese foreign relations as Deng developed his 'open door' policy. In particular, China had developed strong ties with the USA and was working towards a major agreement with the Soviet Union. During the late 1980s, the USA, Japan and the countries of the European Community (EC) had begun a system of 'exchange visits' between high-level military, cultural and economic staff and their opposite numbers in China.

By 1988, China belonged to the World Bank and the International Monetary Fund (IMF), each of which was lending the government large sums of money to spend on economic development. China was also applying to become a member of GATT – an international organization that encouraged free trade between countries.

However, after the crackdown, China's famous 'open door' was banged firmly shut. Within two weeks,

President Bush had suspended all senior staff exchanges with China, and the European Community and Japan soon followed America's lead. The World Bank put a stop to all lending to China, the IMF postponed work on all technical projects, and the negotiations on China's entry into GATT were suspended.

After the crackdown, China received some support from the communist governments of Eastern Europe, who praised the Chinese authorities' firm and decisive action. In particular, the very left-wing government of East Germany congratulated the Deng administration on its suppression of a 'counter-revolutionary rebellion'.

However, by spring 1989 people throughout Eastern Europe were reacting against their rigid communist leaders (see page 40), and a powerful wave of sympathy for the Chinese students swept through most of the communist world. Many expert commentators believe that the crackdown in Tiananmen Square helped to encourage the rebellions in Eastern Europe. These uprisings brought down most of the communist leaders there in the second half of 1989.

China's President Jiang Zemin and US President Bill Clinton wave to reporters during Jiang's visit to Washington DC in 1997.

AFTER THE PROTESTS, THE MOST OBVIOUS CHANGE in China was a tightening of government control. The protest leaders were swiftly rounded up and sent to prison, while many people who had been involved in the demonstrations were given job placements in isolated parts of China. In October 1989, a law controlling mass rallies and demonstrations was passed, and martial law was not lifted in Beijing until January 1990.

The protests did not result in any radical changes in the Chinese government. If anything, the government became more conservative. It continued to be dominated by the elders, led by Premier Li Peng, while Party Secretary Zhao Ziyang, who had spoken out in favour of the students, was immediately replaced by a more committed communist, Jiang Zemin. Jiang had been mayor of Shanghai in the late 1980s and was responsible for the relatively peaceful suppression of student demonstrations there in 1989.

Deng Xiaoping retired from politics in November 1989 but remained a powerful influence in China. At the age of 88, he was still touring the country, campaigning for economic reforms. In 1997, six months after his death, Deng's 'thought' was made part of China's official ideology.

Jiang Zemin became China's state president in 1993. He continued Deng's policy of modernizing China, creating an economy in which businesses could thrive. Under Jiang, China moved steadily towards a more Western-style market economy and most people in China became better off. In 1997 the Chinese took over Hong Kong, a former British colony on the coast of southern China. They continued to run it as a thriving commercial and business centre.

However, China's progress towards modernization has not been accompanied by an increase in democratic freedoms. Long prison sentences are still handed out to anyone who dares to criticize the authorities. China is no closer to holding elections and there is very little freedom of speech or freedom of the press.

Following the world's reaction to the Tiananmen crackdown, the Chinese government became deeply suspicious of foreign countries, especially those in the West. It feared that foreign nations would try to interfere in the way that China was governed and turn the Chinese people against their government. Recently, however, China has begun to restore links with its old foreign partners and is now involved in many international organizations. It has a very important global role to play. The sixth-largest trading nation in the world, China contains one-fifth of the world's population and possesses nuclear weapons. During the past ten years many foreign leaders have visited China, and some have taken the opportunity to speak out on its government's poor record on human rights.

President Clinton and his family stroll along the Great Wall of China in 1998. While he was in China, Clinton took the opportunity to raise questions about the government's record on human rights.

## A New Era

" China still faces enormous difficulties, some of them of its own making: pollution, urban sprawl... the continuing risks of political authoritarianism.... But now... as we look forward to the new millennium, we see a China which has overcome formidable obstacles, which has gone from being the 'sick man of Asia' to being one of the world's largest and fastest developing economies. "

*From* China in the 1990s *by Robert Benewick and Paul Wingrove.*

The city of Shanghai at night. Many of China's cities are now thriving commercial centres.

WHAT MIGHT HAVE HAPPENED IN CHINA IF the Tiananmen crackdown had not taken place? One possibility is that the mood of protest set in motion by the student demonstrations could have become so powerful that it swept through the whole of China, involving not only students but also organized groups of workers. Despite the Chinese government's rigid control, there could have come a moment when the power of the people was just too strong for the authorities to resist. The communist government would have collapsed and elections would have been held for a new, democratic administration.

This is exactly what happened in the communist countries of Eastern Europe at the end of the 1980s. In one country after another, a powerful people's rebellion led to the fall of the communist government and its replacement by a new, democratic system.

Most of these revolts happened in the second half of 1989, after the Tiananmen crackdown, but one major uprising had already taken place in Poland in 1988. There, the powerful and well-organized workers' trade union – Solidarity – organized a mass strike that brought down the government. It was a stunning example of the power of the workers, once they were organized into unions.

The Chinese government was well aware of the threat from workers' unions, and many expert commentators say that it was not the students but the unions that the government was really intent on crushing in 1989.

In Poland, Solidarity members and their supporters gather to protest against the communist government. Their action led to the Polish government's downfall in 1988.

## Crackdown or Chaos?

**" If the way we handled the Tiananmen crisis was incorrect, we would not have today's prosperity. China would be in chaos. The people would have risen and resisted the government. "**

*Zhu Muzhi, President of the China Society for Human Rights Studies (an organization that advises the Chinese government), speaking in 2002.*

So when the government put on a show of force to clear the Square of the students, they were really issuing a much more serious threat to the unions. In the words of an old Chinese proverb they were: 'Killing the chickens to catch the monkey.'

The Tiananmen crackdown could therefore be seen as a clever move on the part of the Chinese government. It frightened off a defenceless group of unarmed students instead of confronting its real enemy, the workers' unions. While the students could be overcome with a minimum of bloodshed, a confrontation with the workers would have been a much more violent affair. This is how the Chinese government has justified its actions.

Another possible outcome of the Tiananmen Square protests could have been that the Chinese government might have listened to the students' demands and begun to make changes in the way China was run. People might have had more right to speak out, the press might have been given more freedom and elections might have been slowly introduced. However, the Chinese government feared that these measures would unleash a flood of protest and unrest and that as a result China would collapse into chaos. Jiang's government claimed it would not have been able to make progress in modernizing China if the country had been in chaos.

Supporters of the Chinese government say that its method of introducing modernization without social freedom has allowed the country to make stunning economic progress. They point to the example of the former Soviet Union, where democratic freedoms were introduced in the early 1990s, but where the economy is in ruins.

People queue for milk in Moscow in 1998. Although Russia has moved towards democracy, many of its people have had to face poverty.

Students arrive in Tiananmen Square in 1998 to protest about human rights abuses. The tradition of protest continues in China, but demonstrations are strictly controlled.

## Not Forgotten

**"** A decade has gone by, but the victims of 1989 are not forgotten. As long as these injustices continue, victims' relatives and campaigners worldwide will keep calling for them to end. **"**

*From a statement issued by the international human rights campaign group, Amnesty International, on the tenth anniversary of the Tiananmen Square crackdown.*

TODAY, PEOPLE IN CHINA RARELY TALK ABOUT THE events of 1989. This is partly the result of the government's determined efforts to suppress all mention of the crackdown, but it is also because the majority of people feel that China has moved on. Most Chinese people see their standard of living rising steadily, and although they realize they have fewer freedoms than the people of other countries, they do not think it worth risking their jobs and security by protesting against the government.

Even today, the Chinese government still keeps a tight control on any discussion of the student protests. Despite repeated appeals from pressure groups inside China and abroad, the government has refused to publish any account of the numbers of people killed, injured or imprisoned in 1989, or to offer any compensation to the victims' families. There are still at least 200 protestors who were taken prisoner in 1989

and have never been released. Those who have been let out of prison have had their movements closely monitored and their freedom restricted. Meanwhile, the number of victims continues to increase as people in China, who campaign for a review of the 1989 events, are arrested for drawing attention to the Tiananmen Square crackdown.

Women soldiers march through Tiananmen Square as part of a massive parade to celebrate the fiftieth anniversary of the communist People's Republic of China. The Chinese are proud of their history and their self-discipline.

Problems continue in Tiananmen Square. Policemen arrest a member of a banned protest movement on New Year's Day, 2001.

In 2001 a set of official government documents on the events of June 1989 was published in a book called *The Tiananmen Papers*. The papers were put together by Zhang Liang, a member of the Jiang government who left China to live in the USA. They contain many official records of the events of June 1989.

The book, which was edited by two American authors, has sold thousands of copies in the West. It has helped people to reassess exactly what happened in the Square by revealing many facts that were previously unknown. However, in China, the news of the publication of *The Tiananmen Papers* led to a new round of arrests, as twenty people were detained by the police on suspicion of smuggling documents out of the country.

Recently there have been a few hopeful signs that the Chinese government's attitude to peaceful protests may be starting to change. In his Government Work Report of 1999, Prime Minister Zhu Rongji instructed troops dealing with protests not to use 'dictatorial means against the people'. This was a direct warning

against the violent treatment of protestors. Meanwhile, another member of the Politburo told the army to listen to public complaints and be patient in its dealings with public discontent.

Zhang Liang says he is confident that the younger wing of the Chinese Communist Party will slowly start to liberalize China. He also believes that the next generation of Chinese leaders will announce a change of attitude to the student movement of the 1980s. If this change really comes about, the Tiananmen Square protest will not have been entirely in vain.

# Glossary

**abdicate**  To give up a position of power.

**activist**  Someone who takes action to make things change.

**Asian Development Bank**  A bank which lends money to help countries in Asia.

**assault rifle**  A type of gun used to attack large groups of people.

**bourgeois**  Interested in material things, and in becoming rich.

**bribery**  The offer of money or a gift in return for doing something.

**capitalism**  A way of organizing a country so that all the land, houses, factories etc. belong to private individuals rather than the state.

**CCP**  The Chinese Communist Party.

**commemorate**  To do something special to remember a person or an event.

**communism**  A way of organizing a country so that all the land, houses, factories etc. belong to the state and the profits are shared among everyone.

**communist**  Someone who believes in communism.

**congress**  A large meeting (as in Communist Party congress).

**conservative**  Cautious, and keen to keep things as they are.

**counter-revolutionary**  Against the revolution. (The Chinese government used this term to suggest that the student activities were against the spirit of the original communist revolution that overthrew the emperor of China.)

**crackdown**  A strong action intended to stop something from happening.

**cudgel**  A thick stick, used for beating someone.

**democracy**  A way of governing a country, in which the people choose their leaders in elections.

**democratic**  Giving everyone equal rights.

**detain**  To keep a person in prison for a while.

**dialogue**  Two-way discussion.

**editorial (as in newspaper editorial)**  Written comments on events in the news.

**elders**  The name given to a group of mainly older Chinese politicians, who were very powerful in the 1980s and 1990s.

**European Community (EC)**  A group of countries in Europe that had special trade and political agreements with each other. The EC has now been renamed the EU (European Union).

**GATT**  An international organization that encourages trade between nations. The initials stand for the General Agreement on Tariffs and Trade.

**hard labour**  Very hard, physical work.

**hardliner**  Someone who is not moderate and will not change their mind.

**hospital drip**  A bag containing blood or some other fluid which is slowly pumped through a tube into a patient's body.

**hostel**  A large building in which students, or other people, live.

**human rights**  The right of all people to have justice, fair treatment and free speech.

**ideology**  A set of ideas that someone believes in.

**intellectuals**  People who think hard about the world and share their ideas with others, through discussion and writing.

**International Monetary Fund (IMF)**  An international organization set up to encourage trade between nations.

**Kuomintang**  A Chinese political party founded in 1911 that overthrew the emperor. The Kuomintang is now the ruling party in Taiwan.

**left wing**  In favour of workers' rights and the equal sharing out of wealth.

**liberal**  Tolerant and accepting of other people's ideas.

**market economy**  A way of running a country which is led by what people want to buy.

**martial law**  Control of a country by the army.

**paramount**  Most important.

**party secretary** A very important position in the Chinese government. The party secretary is the leader of the government but is under the control of the Paramount Ruler.

**peasant** Someone who works on the land. Peasants are usually very poor.

**petition** A written request for something, usually signed by many people.

**PLA** The People's Liberation Army, the army of the Chinese government.

**point-blank** Very close up.

**Politburo** The decision-making part of the Chinese government.

**radical** Very extreme.

**rallies** Large meetings.

**republic** A country or state that does not have a king or queen.

**rickshaw** A two-wheeled passenger vehicle pulled by one or two men.

**Security Bureau** A department of the Chinese government that is responsible for making sure that the country stays peaceful.

**slogans** Short messages.

**social reform** Changes in the way a country is run.

**stalemate** A position in an argument or some other form of conflict in which both sides are stuck, and neither can make a move.

**status** Someone's position in society.

**Styrofoam** A form of very light plastic.

**trade union** An organized group of workers, set up to improve working conditions and pay.

**underground (as in magazines/pamphlets)** Published and spread secretly.

**work placement** A job that is found for someone.

**World Bank** An international organization set up to help developing nations, usually by providing loans.

# Further Information

## Books for Younger Readers

*China: The Culture* by Bobbie Kalman (Crabtree, 2000)

*China Under Communism* by Michael G. Kort (Millbrook Press, 1995)

*The Rise of Modern China* by Tony Allan (Heinemann Library, 2002)

*The Tiananmen Square Massacre*, edited by Kelly Barth (Greenhaven Press, 2002)

## Books for Older Readers

*Tiananmen Diary: Thirteen Days in June* by Harrison E. Salisbury (Unwin Paperbacks, 1989)

*The Tiananmen Papers: The Chinese Leadership's Decision to Use Force Against Their Own People – In Their Own Words* compiled by Zhang Liang, edited by Andrew J. Nathan and Perry Link (Abacus, 2001)

*Lili: A Novel of Tiananmen* by Annie Wang (Random House, 2001)

*Red China Blues: My Long March from Mao to Now* by Jan Wong (Doubleday, 1997)

## Films

*The Gate of Heavenly Peace* (producers Richard Gordon and Carma Hinton, PBS, 1994).

# Timeline

**221** BCE  Qin Shi Huangdhi, the first emperor of China, unites China and starts a tradition of very strict rule.

**c.1400** CE  The Ming emperors begin to build The Forbidden City in Beijing.

**1800s**  The Chinese government fights European traders for control of Chinese trade.

**1911**  The Kuomintang starts a revolution in China.

**1912**  The last emperor of China abdicates.

**1919**  May 4 Movement takes place, a student protest in Tiananmen Square against the terms of the Treaty of Versailles made at the end of the First World War.

**1920**  The Communist Party is founded.

**1934**  The Long March, led by Mao Tse-tung, prevents the Communist Party from being wiped out.

**1949**  Mao Tse-tung announces the start of the People's Republic of China in Tiananmen Square. Mao starts the Great Leap Forward.

**1966**  Mao starts the Cultural Revolution.

**1976**  Mao Tse-tung dies and the Gang of Four are arrested.

**Autumn 1978**  Students set up a Democracy Wall in Beijing.

**December 1978**  Deng Xiaoping takes control of China. He soon begins his four modernizations.

**1985**  Mikhail Gorbachev becomes leader of the Soviet Union and begins to introduce social reforms.

**November 1986**  Student demonstrations take place against the government in many Chinese cities.

**January 1987**  Government cracks down on student protests.

**15 April 1989**  Death of Hu Yaobang, the former party secretary, leads to an outbreak of protests.

**22 April 1989**  Three student representatives present a petition to Premier Li Peng. On the same day there are violent demonstrations in the city of Xi'an.

**26 April 1989**  Government editorial in the *People's Daily* condemning the student demonstrators.

**4 May 1989**  Student demonstration in Tiananmen Square marks the anniversary of the May 4 Movement.

**13 May 1989**  Hundreds of students in Tiananmen Square announce a hunger strike.

**17 May 1989**  President Gorbachev arrives in Beijing for talks with the Chinese government.

**20 May 1989**  Premier Li Peng declares martial law in parts of Beijing. The announcement leads to demonstrations all over China.

**2 June 1989**  A new hunger strike is announced in Tiananmen Square. Some PLA troops start marching towards the Square.

**3 June 1989**  Troops surround Tiananmen Square. Some clashes take place in and around the Square.

**4 June 1989**  Crackdown. Tiananmen Square is emptied of students. Shooting and riots in the streets of Beijing.

**August 1989**  Poland ceases to be a communist country and holds democratic elections for its leaders.

**October 1989**  In response to demonstrations in many parts of China, the government passes a law controlling mass rallies and demonstrations.

**November 1989**  Deng Xiaoping retires from politics. Jiang Zemin becomes China's state president.

**2001**  A set of government documents on the events of 1989 are published in *The Tiananmen Papers*.

In 1999 improvements costing twelve million dollars were made to Tiananmen Square. Here, visitors flock to the newly re-opened site.